A SHORT
HISTORY
OF
BUDDHISM

Edward Conze

ONEWORLD
OXFORD

A Short History of Buddhism

Oneworld Publications
(Sales and Editorial)
185 Banbury Road
Oxford OX2 7AR, England

Oneworld Publications
(U.S. Marketing Office)
P O Box 830, 21 Broadway
Rockport, MA 01966
U.S.A.

This new edition published by Oneworld Publications 1993
Reprinted 1995 and 1996

A CIP record for this book is available from the British Library

ISBN 1-85168-066-7

Printed and bound in Great Britain by
Guernsey Press, Guernsey

CONTENTS

CHAPTER 3 THE THIRD PERIOD: AD 500–1000

CHAPTER 4 THE LAST ONE THOUSAND YEARS: AD 1000–1978

INTRODUCTION

THE
HISTORICAL CONTEXT
AND THE
EPOCHS OF BUDDHIST HISTORY

A. Buddhism claims that a person called "The Buddha", or "The Enlightened One", rediscovered a very ancient and long-standing, in fact an ageless, wisdom, and that he did so in Bihar in India, round about 600 or 400 BC — the exact date is unknown. His re-formulation of the perennial wisdom was designed to counteract three evils.

> 1. *Violence* had to be avoided in all its forms, from the killing of humans and animals to the intellectual coercion of those who think otherwise.
> 2. The *"self"*, or the fact that one holds on to oneself as an individual personality, was held to be responsible for all pain and suffering, which would in the end be finally abolished by the attainment of a state of self-extinction, technically known as "Nirvana".
> 3. *Death* was an error which could be overcome by those who entered the "doors to the Deathless", "the gates of the Undying".

Apart from providing antidotes to these three ills, the Buddha formulated no definite doctrines or creeds, but put his entire trust into the results obtained by training his disciples through a threefold process of moral restraint, secluded meditation and philosophical reflection.

As to the first point, that of *violence* – the technical term for "non-violence" is *ahimsá*, which means the avoidance of harm to all life. In this respect Buddhism was one of the many movements which reacted against the technological tyrannies which had arisen about 3000 BC, whose technical projects and military operations had led to widespread and often senseless violence and destruction of life.

From its very beginning the growth of civilization has been accompanied by recurrent waves of disillusion with power and material wealth. About 600 BC onwards one such wave swept through the whole of Asia, through all parts of it, from China to the Greek islands on the coast of Asia Minor, mobilizing the resources of the spirit against the existing power system.

In India the reaction arose in a region devoted to rice culture, as distinct from the areas further West with their animal husbandry and cultivation of wheat. For the last two thousand years Buddhism has mainly flourished in rice-growing countries and little elsewhere. In addition, and that is much harder to explain, it has spread only into those countries which had previously had a cult of Serpents or Dragons, and never made headway in those parts of the world which view the killing of dragons as a meritorious deed or blame serpents for mankind's ills.

As to the second point, concerning the *self*, in offering a cure for individualism Buddhism addresses itself to an individualistic city population. It arose in a part of India where, round Benares and Patna, the iron age had thrown up ambitious warrior kings, who had established large kingdoms, with big cities, widespread trade, a fairly developed money economy and a rationally organized state. These cities replaced small-scale tribal societies by large-scale conurbations, with all the evils of depersonalization, specialization and social disorganization that that entails.

2

Most of the Buddha's public activity took place in cities and that helps to account for the intellectual character of his teachings, the "urbanity" of his utterances and the rational quality of his ideas. The Buddha always stressed that he was a guide, not an authority, and that all propositions must be tested, including his own. Having had the advantage of a liberal education, the Buddhists react to the unproven with a benevolent scepticism and so they have been able to accommodate themselves to every kind of popular belief, not only in India, but in all countries they moved into.

As to the third point, concerning *death*; there is something here which we do not quite understand. The Buddha obviously shared the conviction, widely held in the early stages of mankind's history, that death is not a necessary ingredient of our human constitution, but a sign that something has gone wrong with us. It is our own fault; essentially we are immortal and can conquer death and win eternal life by religious means. The Buddha attributed death to an evil force, called *Mára*, "the Killer", who tempts us away from our true immortal selves and diverts us from the path which could lead us back to freedom. On the principle that "it is the lesser part which dies" we are tied to Mára's realm through our cravings and through our attachment to an individual personality which is their visible embodiment. In shedding our attachments we move beyond "death's realm", "beyond the death-king's sight" and win relief from an endless series of repeated deaths, which each time rob us of the loot of a lifetime.

B. Buddhism has so far persisted for about 2,500 years and during that period it has undergone profound and radical changes. Its history can conveniently be divided into four periods. The first period is that of the old Buddhism, which largely coincided with what later came to be known as the "Hínayána"; the second is marked by the rise of the Maháyána; the third by that of the Tantra and Ch'an. This brings us to about AD 1000. After that Buddhism no longer renewed itself, but just persisted, and the last 1,000 years can be taken together as the fourth period.

Geographically, first period Buddhism remained almost purely Indian; during the second period it started on its conquest of Eastern Asia and was in its turn considerably influenced by non-Indian thought; during the third, creative centres of Buddhist thought were established outside India, particularly in China. Philosophically, the first period concentrated on psychological questions, the second on ontological, the third on cosmic. The first is concerned with individuals gaining control over their own minds, and psychological analysis is the method by which self-control is sought; the second turns to the nature (svabháva) of true reality and the realization in oneself of that true nature of things is held to be decisive for salvation; the third sees adjustment and harmony with the cosmos as the clue to enlightenment and uses age-old magical and occult methods to achieve it. Soteriologically, they differ in the conception of the type of man they try to produce. In the first period the ideal saint is an Arhat, or a person who has non-attachment, in whom all craving is extinct and who will no more be reborn in this world. In the second it is the Bodhisattva, a person who wishes to save all his fellow-beings and who hopes ultimately to become an omniscient Buddha. In the third it is a Siddha, a man who is so much in harmony with the cosmos that he is under no constraint whatsoever and as a free agent is able to manipulate the cosmic forces both inside and outside himself.

Other religions may perhaps have undergone changes as startling as these, but what is peculiar to Buddhism is that the

innovations of each new phase were backed up by the production of a fresh canonical literature which, although clearly
composed many centuries after the Buddha's death, claims to be
the word of the Buddha Himself. The Scriptures of the first
period were supplemented in the second by a large number of
Maháyána Sútras and in the third by a truly enormous number of
Tantras. All these writings are anonymous in the sense that their
authors are unknown and the claim that they were all spoken by
the Buddha Himself involves, as we shall see (ch. 2 sec. 1), a
rather elastic conception of the Buddha.

At any given time the newer developments did not entirely
supersede the older ones. The older schools coexisted with the
new ones, although they were often profoundly modified by
them. The old Buddhism of the first period absorbed in the
second a good many of the tenets of the Maháyána and the
contact between the Tantras and the Maháyána led to a
synthesis which took place in the universities of Bengal and
Orissa during the Pála period (see ch. 3 sec. 1). In my account I
will concentrate on the creative impulses and they will be my
guide.

The division of Buddhist history into periods of 500 years
does not only agree with the facts, but it is mentioned in many
Buddhist writings dating from the beginning of the Christian era.
These five periods of 500 years are enumerated as marking the
continued degeneration of the doctrine. Like everything else, the
Buddhist order and doctrine is bound to decay, in each period its
spirituality will be diminished, and after 2,500 years it will be near
its extinction (see ch. 4 sec. 9). Whether or not observation bears
out this diagnosis of a continuous decay, it had a profound
influence on the mentality of the Buddhists in later ages, and we
will hear of it again and again. The story of Buddhism is indeed
not only a splendid, but also a melancholy one.

To the modern historian, Buddhism is a phenomenon which must exasperate him at every point and we can only say in extenuation that this religion was not founded for the benefit of historians. Not only is there an almost complete absence of hard facts about its history in India; not only is the date, authorship and geographical provenance of the overwhelming majority of the documents almost entirely unknown, but even its doctrines must strike the historian as most unsatisfactory, and elusive. Buddhists tend to cancel out each statement by a counter-statement and the truth is obtained not by choosing between the two contradictory statements, but by combining them. What then, apart from their characteristic terminology, is common to all this variety of diverse teachings, what are the common factors which allow us to call all of them "Buddhist"?

1. Among the more stable factors the *monastic organization* is the most obvious and conspicuous. Its continuity is the basis which supports everything else (see ch. 1 sec. 2).

2. Next we have as a constant element a traditional set of *meditations* which have moulded all generations of Buddhists and which are bound to exert a fairly uniform effect on everyone who subjects himself to their influence (see ch. 1 sec. 3).

3. Thirdly, all Buddhists have had one and the same *aim*, which is the "extinction of self", the dying out of separate individuality, and their teachings and practices have generally tended to foster such easily recognizable spiritual *virtues* as serenity, detachment, consideration and tenderness for others. In the Scriptures, the Dharma has been compared to a *taste*. The word of the Buddha is there defined as that which has the taste of Peace, the taste of Emancipation, the taste of Nirvana. It is, of course, a peculiarity of tastes that they are not easily

described, and must elude those who refuse actually to taste them for themselves.

4. Throughout its history, Buddhism has the unity of an *organism*, in that each new development takes place in continuity from the previous one. Nothing could look more different from a tadpole than a frog and yet they are stages of the same animal, and evolve continuously from each other. The Buddhist capacity for metamorphosis must astound those who only see the end-products separated by long intervals of time, as different as chrysalis and butterfly. In fact they are connected by many gradations, which lead from one to the other and which only close study can detect. There is in Buddhism really no innovation, but what seems so is in fact a subtle adaptation of pre-existing ideas. Great attention has always been paid to continuous doctrinal development and to the proper transmission of the teachings. These are not the anarchic philosophizings of individualists who strive for originality at all costs. Instead, we have groups of teachers, known as "sects" or "schools", and lines of masters which maintain continuity over many centuries.

CHAPTER

1

THE
FIRST FIVE HUNDRED YEARS
500–0 BC

1 THE PECULIARITIES OF THE FIRST PERIOD

The absence of hard facts is particularly marked for the first period. One, and only one, date is really certain and that is the rule of the emperor Aśoka (274–236) whose patronage transformed Buddhism from a small sect of ascetics into an all-Indian religion. Even the date of the Buddha's life is a matter of conjecture. Indian tradition often tells us that His death took place 100 years before Aśoka. Modern scholars have on the whole agreed to place His life between 563 and 483 BC. With some reluctance I have here followed their chronology.

The nature of our documents gives rise to further uncertainties. During this entire period the Scriptures were transmitted orally and they were written down only towards the end of it. Of the actual words of the Buddha nothing is left. The Buddha may have taught in Ardhamagadhi, but none of His sayings is preserved in its original form. As for the earliest Canon, even its language is still a matter of dispute. All we have are translations of what may have been the early Canon into other Indian languages, chiefly Páli and a particular form of Buddhist Sanskrit. Always without a central organization, Buddhism had divided itself at some unspecified time into a number of sects, of which usually eighteen are counted. Most of these sects had their own Canon. Nearly all of them are lost to us, either

because they were never written down, or because the depreda-
tions of time have destroyed the written record. Only those are
left which after the collapse of Buddhism in India about AD
1200 had by some chance got into some region outside India,
like Ceylon, Nepal, or Central Asia, or which had been previously translated into Chinese or Tibetan. We therefore possess
only a small portion of what actually circulated in the Buddhist
community during the first period. What is more, the selection
of what is preserved is due more to chance than considerations
of antiquity and intrinsic merit.

And that which we have may have been composed at any
time during the first five hundred years. First of all it must
state quite clearly that there is no objective criterion which
would allow us to single out those elements in the record
which go back to the Buddha Himself. Some modern
European books abound in confident assertions about what the
Buddha Himself has personally taught. They are all mere
guesswork. The "original gospel" is beyond our ken now. The
farthest we can get back in time is the period when the
community split up into separate sects. What we can do is to
compare the documents of the various sects, say a Theravádin
Dhammapáda from Ceylon with a Sarvástivádin *Udánavarga*
found in the sands of Turkestan. Where we find passages in
which these two texts, the one in Páli and the other in
Sanskrit, agree word by word, we can assume that they belong
to a time antedating the separation of the two schools, which
took place during Aśoka's rule. Where they do not agree, we
may infer their post-Aśokan date in the absence of evidence to
the contrary. So far no one has yet systematically undertaken
such a comparison and until that is done we are unable to
clearly distinguish the doctrines of the first one or two
centuries, from those of post-Aśokan times. It is not even quite

9

certain when and under what circumstances these separations of the sects took place, since all the works we have on the subject are five centuries later than the events they report and the data are everywhere distorted by sectarian bias. But whether our knowledge gets us to within one century of the neighbourhood of the Nirvana, or to within two or three centuries only, there is an initial period which is shrouded in mystery and to which we cannot penetrate.

In the next two sections I will try to explain the doctrines which marked the Buddhism of the first period as far as it can be inferred with some probability. They first concern monastic discipline, and then the basic theory of salvation and the way to it.

2 THE MONASTIC DISCIPLINE

The oldest documents which we can place with some degree of certainty before Aśoka happen to deal with monastic discipline (Vinaya). From fairly early times onwards the traditions concerning the Buddha's teachings were grouped under two principal headings called respectively Dharma and Vinaya. The Vinaya proved the more stable and uniform element of the two, much less subject to disagreements and re-formulations. Discussions on the Vinaya are seldom heard of and even at later times school formations rarely implied modifications in the Vinaya, except in quite external and superficial matters, such as dress, etc. Even when with the Maháyána quite new schools arose on dogmatic grounds, they adhered for a long time as far as the Vinaya was concerned to one of the older Hínayána schools. In actual practice there has been, of course, much plain disregard of the more onerous rules in the long history of the order, but as for their formulation it seems to have reached its final form already in the fourth century BC. At that time a great work, the *Skandhaka*, was produced, which divided and arranged the enormous material accumulated by then according to a well conceived plan. It regulates the fundamental institutions of Buddhist monastic life, the admission to the order, the confession ceremonies, the retirement during the rainy season, and it discusses clothing, food and drugs for the sick, as well as the rules to be observed in the punishment of offenders.

Older still are the approximately two hundred and fifty rules of the *Prátimoksha*, a classification of ecclesiastical offences, of which we possess about a dozen different recensions, which agree on all essentials. These rules must be recited every fortnight in front of a chapter of the monks. Among all the texts of the Scriptures there is none that has enjoyed among Buddhists an authority as uncontested, widespread and lasting as these Prátimoksha rules, and it is therefore necessary to give the reader some idea of their contents.

First of all they list four offences which deserve expulsion, i.e. sexual intercourse, theft, murder, and the false claim to either supernatural powers of high spiritual attainments. Then follow thirteen lighter offences, which deserve suspension, and of which five concern sexual misconduct, two the building of huts, and the remaining six dissensions within the Order. The recitation then continues to enumerate two sexual offences which are "punishable according to the circumstances", and after that come thirty offences which "involve forfeiture" of the right to share in garments belonging to the Order and which, in addition, make the offender liable to an unfavourable rebirth. They forbid, among other things, the handling of gold and silver as well as trading activities, or the personal appropriation of goods intended for the community. Next there are ninety offences which, unless repented and expiated, will be punished by an unfavourable rebirth. They concern such things as telling lies, belittling or slandering other monks, they regulate the relations with the laity by forbidding "to teach the Scriptures word by word to an unordained person", to tell laymen about the offences committed by monks, and so on. For the rest they concern a huge variety of misde-meanours, e.g. they forbid to destroy any kind of vegetation, to dig the earth, to drink alcoholic beverages, or to have a chair or bed made with legs higher than eight inches. The obviously very archaic document then further gives four offences requiring confession, followed by thirteen rules of decorum, and it concludes with seven rules for the settling of disputes.

The purpose of the Vinaya rules was to provide ideal condi-tions for meditation and renunciation. They try to enforce a complete withdrawal from social life, a separation from its interests and worries, and the rupture of all ties with family or clan. At the same time the insistence on extreme simplicity and frugality was meant to ensure independence, while the giving up of home and all property was intended to foster non-attach-ment. Originally, the Order seems to have been conceived as composed of wandering beggars, who ate food obtained as alms in their begging bowls, wore clothes made from rags picked up on rubbish heaps and dwelt in the forest, in caves or at the foot of trees. Only during the rainy season must they cease roaming about and stay in one and the same place. At all times a minority continued to aspire after the rigours of this primitive simplicity, but, generally speaking, with the increas-ing prosperity of the religion the monks settled down in monasteries which gave aloofness from social concerns without some of the inconveniences of the hand-to-mouth existence originally envisaged. The text of the Vinaya being fixed once and for all, its further history is one of constant compromises between its sacrosanct provisions on the one hand, and social realities and human fallibility on the other.

3 THE BASIC DOCTRINES

So much about the practices of the monks. What then were the doctrines common to all the Buddhists of the first period, and shared not only by them but by all later Buddhists however much they might modify them by additions and reservations? They can be grouped under two main headings. They first of all propound a *theory of salvation*, showing the need for it, its nature and the methods necessary to attain it. They secondly concern the *three "Jewels"* or *"Treasures"*, i.e. the Buddha, the Dharma and the Samgha.

In its core, Buddhism is a *doctrine of salvation*. The need for it arises from the hopelessly unsatisfactory character of the world in which we find ourselves. Buddhists take an extremely gloomy view of the conditions in which we have the misfortune to live. It is particularly the impermanence of everything in and around us that suggests the worthlessness of our worldly aspirations which in the nature of things can never lead to any lasting achievement or abiding satisfaction. In the end death takes away everything we managed to pile up and parts us from everything we cherished. How futile is the search for security in such surroundings, for happiness with such unsuitable materials! The joys and pleasures of the children of the world are exceedingly trivial and their choices and preferences betray little wisdom. They behave rather like the small child who finds a marble of exceeding beauty with a green spot on it, is overjoyed at having found it, and who, so as to make quite sure of not losing it again, proceeds straightaway to swallow the marble, with the result that his stomach has to be pumped out. Further, who would not be frightened if he realized all the pains and terrors to which he exposes himself by having a body! Suffering without end in a futile round of rebirths after rebirths (*samsára*), that is the lot of ordinary people and the revulsion from it is the spur to salvation. The Buddhist ascetics were men who in fear of birth and death had left home life to gain salvation.

If next we ask for the cause of this unsatisfactory state of affairs, we are told that it is not imposed upon us by any outside force, by some fate or malevolent deity, but that it is due to some factor in our own mental constitution. This factor is variously described as "craving", the "belief in a separate self", "ignorance" or adherence to the "perverted views". Not only the craving for sense-pleasures, for money, social position or power is apt to put us in bondage to the forces which we vainly hope to use for our own ends, but any form of desire whatsoever is condemned by Buddhists as destructive of our inward freedom and independence. From another angle we may say that the whole of our unhappiness stems from the habit of trying to appropriate some part of the universe as if it were our "own" and to say of as many things as we can that "this is mine, I am this, this is myself". It is a fundamental teaching of Buddhism that this word "self" does not correspond to a real fact, that the self is fictitious and that therefore by our self-seeking we sacrifice our true welfare to a mere fiction. Finally, Buddhism differs from Christianity in that it sees the root cause of all evil in "ignorance" and not in "sin", in an act of intellectual misapprehension and not in an act of volition and rebellion. As a working definition of ignorance we are offered the four "perverted views" (*viparyása*) which make us seek for permanence in what is inherently impermanent, ease in what is inseparable from suffering, selfhood in what is not linked to any self, and delight in what is essentially repulsive and disgusting.

The situation would, of course, be entirely hopeless if this world of suffering and Samsára comprised the whole extent of reality. In fact this is not so, and beyond it there is something else, which is called Nirvana, a transcendental state which is quite beyond the ken of ordinary experience, and of which nothing can be said except that in it all ills have ceased, together with their causes and consequences. Buddhists are less intent on defining this Nirvana, than on realizing it within themselves. And they are very much averse to making positive statements about the man who has gone to Nirvana. This world is often compared to a house on fire, which everyone in his senses will try to escape from. But if the samsaric world is like a fire, then Nirvana is like the state which results from the extinction of that fire. As we read in the *Sutta Nipáta* (1074, 1079), one of our more ancient texts:

> As flame flung on by force of wind
> Comes to its end, reaches what none
> Can sum; the silent sage, released,
> From name-and-form, goes to the goal,
> Reaches the state that none can sum.
> When all conditions are removed,
> All ways of telling also are removed.

Since the causes of all evil lie within ourselves, we ourselves can, by our own efforts, rid ourselves of them, if we only know how to go about it. Like a good physician the Buddha has given us a profusion of remedies for the great variety of our ailments. On their lower levels the Buddhist methods of salvation are similar to those found in other religions. A man must first of all bring some *morality* into his daily life, and he must observe the "five precepts" which forbid killing, stealing, sexual misconduct, lying and the use of intoxicants. Next he must take care how he earns his living. Butchers, fishermen, or soldiers, for instance, break the first precept all the time, and little spirituality can be expected of them. Other occupations are less perilous to the soul, but the safest and most fruitful is that of a homeless and propertyless monk who relies on others for all his material needs.

But once the moral foundations are laid, the remainder of the Buddhist efforts consist in mental training, in *meditations* of various kinds. Meditation is a mental training which is carried out for three distinct, but interconnected, purposes:

1. It aims at a withdrawal of attention from its normal preoccupation with constantly changing sensory stimuli and ideas centred on oneself.

2. It aims at effecting a shift of attention from the sensory world to another, subtler realm, thereby calming the turmoils of the mind. Sense-based knowledge is as inherently unsatisfactory as a sense-based life. Sensory and historical facts as such are uncertain, unfruitful, trivial, and largely a matter of indifference. Only that is worth knowing which is discovered in meditation, when the doors of the senses are closed. The truths of this holy religion must elude the average worldling with his sense-based knowledge, and his sense-bounded horizon.

3. It aims at penetrating into the suprasensory reality itself, at roaming about among the transcendental facts, and this quest leads it to Emptiness as the one ultimate reality.

In Buddhist terminology, the first preliminary step is known as "mindfulness" (*smrti*), which is followed then by "ecstatic trance" (*samádhi*) and "wisdom" (*prajñá*). The relation of the three is indicated by the following diagram:

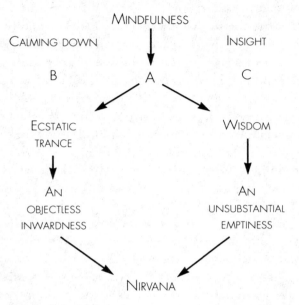

MINDFULNESS

CALMING DOWN   INSIGHT

B   A   C

ECSTATIC TRANCE   WISDOM

AN OBJECTLESS INWARDNESS   AN UNSUBSTANTIAL EMPTINESS

NIRVANA

This is the classification of the meditations according to their purpose. From another point of view they can be classified according to their subjects or topics. A considerable number of such topics were offered to the aspirant, and his choice among them depends on his mental endowments and proclivities. So vast is the range of possibilities offered that they cannot possibly be even enumerated here. There we have relatively simple breathing exercises of the Yogic type, a survey of the "thirty-two parts of the body", the contemplation of corpses in various degrees of decomposition, an introspective awareness of our mental processes as they go along, be they feelings, thoughts, or the hindrances to concentration, or the factors which make for enlightenment. Then there is the cultivation of the social emotions, such as friendliness and compassion, the recollection of the virtues of the three Jewels, the meditation on death and the aspiration for Nirvana. A favourite subject of meditation are the twelve links of the chain of conditioned co-production (*pratítya-samutpáda*), which shows how ignorance leads to the other factors of worldly existence ending in old age and death and how, conversely, the extinction of ignorance must lead to the extinction of all these factors. Other meditations again try to impress on our minds the facts of the impermanence of all conditioned things, to show up the full extent of suffering, demonstrate the inanity of the term "self", to foster insight into emptiness and to reveal the characteristic features of the path which leads to salvation. In fact, there seems to be almost no limit to the number of meditational devices which are attested for the first period of Buddhism, although it was apparently only in the second period that some systematic order was imposed upon them.

Now as to the *Three Jewels*. *The Buddha* is essential to this religion as its founder who guarantees the truth and reliability of the teaching by the fact that He is "fully enlightened". He has awoken to the nature and meaning of life and has found a definite way out of it. He differs from all other people in that He has by Himself found the truth, and that He knows everything that is necessary to salvation. Whether He knew also all other things, i.e. whether he was omniscient in the full sense of the term, was a matter of dispute among the sects. There was, however, general agreement that He knew everything needful for the attainment of final peace and that therefore He could in spiritual matters act as a sure and infallible guide.

The word "Buddha" itself is, of course, not a proper name but a title, or epithet, which means the "Enlightened One". It refers to the condition of a man who was a completely unobstructed channel for the spiritual force of Dharma, or Reality. The personal name of the historical Buddha was Gautama, or Siddhártha, and after His tribe He is often called Śákyamuni, "the sage from the tribe of the Śákyas". With the historical individual the Buddhist religion is not greatly concerned. His value to the religion lay in His transmission of the spiritual teachings about Dharma. A duality of this kind is normal in authoritative Asian religious leaders. In recent years we have met it again in Mohandas Karamchand Gándhi, who at the same time was the Mahátma, the "Great-souled One", a word for the spiritual force which worked through that particular individual.

In this way the individual, called Gautama or Śákyamuni, somehow coexists with the spiritual principle of Buddhahood, which is variously called the "Tathágata", or "the Dharmabody" or "the Buddha-nature". The Buddhists have, however, always maintained that the exact relation between His individual and His spiritual sides cannot be defined. They have also consistently opposed the tendencies of the unregenerate to put their faith into a living actual person and have done everything to belittle the importance of the Buddha's actual physical existence. It is the Buddha Himself who is reported to have said to Vakkali: "What is there, Vakkali, in seeing this vile body of mine? Whoso sees the spiritual Law, or Dharma, he sees me; whoso sees me sees the spiritual Dharma. Seeing Dharma, Vakkali, he sees me; seeing me, he sees Dharma."

As the manifestation of a type, the "historical Buddha" is not an isolated phenomenon, but one of a series of Buddhas who appear in this world throughout the ages. Knowledge of the non-historical Buddhas seems to have grown as time went on. Originally there were seven, then we hear of twenty-four, and so the number steadily increased. The "seven Buddhas", i.e. Śákyamuni and His six predecessors, are frequently represented

19

in art – in Bharhut and Sanchi by Their stúpas and Bodhi-trees, in Gandhara, Mathura and Ajanta during our second period in human form, each nearly indistinguishable from the other. It was only towards the end of the first period that interest shifted to two other non-historical Buddhas. With the development of the Bodhisattva-theory (see ch. 2 sec. 1) comes Dípankara, Śákyamuni's twenty-fourth predecessor, under whom He first resolved to become a Buddha. With the spread of pessimism about the continued vitality of Śákyamuni's message comes the cult of Maitreya, the future Buddha, under whom the Dharma will reappear with new vigour.

This period had little interest in the biography of the Buddha Śákyamuni as a person. It would be difficult to reconstruct the facts of His life from the details we have. Interest concentrated on the two periods of His life which had the greatest significance for the believer, i.e. to the period of His enlightenment which marked His victory over ignorance, and to His last days, when He attained His final Nirvana, and consummated His victory over death and the world. For the rest it appears that the greater part of what we believe to know of His life was at first a part of the Vinaya tradition, that it consisted of an account which began with His genealogy and miraculous birth, and went on beyond His final Nirvana to the legendary first Council of Rájagrha where the Canon of the Sacred Scriptures is said to have been compiled, and ended with the so-called second council of Vaiśali where controversial points of disciplinary practice were discussed. The story of His life was at first a collection of precedents, which were invoked to justify the Vinaya rules. In addition, many stories and legends gradually grew up in connection with some holy place or shrine, to account for its sanctity. Little attempt was made to weave all these stories into one consecutive biography. At present we are not in a position to decide which ones of them are trustworthy historical information and which ones are the pious inventions of a later age. Nothing was in any case more alien to the mentality of the monks of this first period than to make such distinctions between these two orders of facts.

Our description of the Buddha would be incomplete if we failed to mention that alone among mortals of His age He had in addition to His normal physical body, as it appeared to common people, still a kind of "ethereal" body, which only the elect could see with the eye of faith and which Buddhist art tried to reproduce to the best of its abilities. The "ethereal" body is sixteen feet high, and it possesses the thirty-two "marks of the superman". For instance, the Buddhas have wheels engraved on Their feet, webs between Their fingers, a cowl on Their heads, a halo and an aureole round Their heads and bodies, a tuft of white curly hair between Their eyebrows, and so on and so on. In the form in which we have it, this tradition is obviously post-Aśokan. Parts of it may, however, go back much further, to ancient and even pre-Buddhist traditions about manly beauty, and to the age-old art of predicting a person's destiny, nature and future from such signs and prognostics.

A Buddha's body differs from that of other people not only by the possession of the thirty-two marks, but in addition it has the peculiar property that its bony parts are indestructible. At the cremation of the Buddha Śákyamuni they were not reduced to ashes, and they formed the *relics* which were distributed among the believers, and were preserved from generation to generation, like the Buddha's tooth now in Kandy.

Dharma, the second of these Treasures, comprises all the mysteries of the Buddhist faith, and cannot easily be explained in a few words. Buddhists in Asia normally did not describe themselves as "Buddhists", but as "followers of the Dharma". This

"Dharma" is the name for an impersonal spiritual force behind and in everything. Being spiritual and not of this world, it is rather elusive and not easy to define or get hold of. Judged by logical standards the word is extremely ambiguous. But since the Dharma is the subject-matter of all Buddhist teachings, it is necessary to list its main meanings, and to show their interconnection:

1. First of all it is a word for the *one ultimate reality*. One spiritual reality underlies all that we perceive in and around us. It is real as contrasted with the illusory things of the common-sense world, to it we should turn as we should turn away from them, for it alone brings true satisfaction. And it is not external to worldly things and events, but in some ways immanent to them, and the directing Law within them.

2. Secondly, by an easy transition, it means that ultimate reality as interpreted or stated in the Buddha's teaching, and in this subjective form it means *"Doctrine"*, "Scripture", or "Truth".

3. Thirdly, Dharma, in both the first and second sense, may be reflected in our lives, may manifest itself in our actions, insofar as we act in accordance with it. The word thus assumes the meaning of *"righteousness"* and "virtue".

4. It is in its fourth sense that the word becomes rather subtle and assumes a meaning which constitutes the specific contribution of Buddhist thought, containing at the same time within it all the tensions that have caused it to develop. Buddhist writings everywhere are replete with references to *"dharmas"* in the plural and they become unintelligible unless the specific meaning of this term is appreciated. The word is here used in a scientific sense, which results from considering things and events in their relation to the Dharma in sense 1, i.e. from studying them as they are in their own ultimate reality. Nearly

all scientific and philosophical systems agree in rejecting the
appearance of the commonsense world as a false artificial construction, replacing it by an explanation of events based on
intelligible entities of various kinds. The most obvious example
is the atomic system. Behind the sensory appearance of the
material world this system postulates another world, composed
of atoms, fairly invisible and adequately grasped only by math-
ematical formulas. These atoms are that which is physically
really there, a thorough understanding of their behaviour
allows us to control the physical universe, and we can deduce
from them the physical properties of things which our senses
perceive. Likewise, the Buddhists assume that our common-
sense view of the world is hopelessly distorted by ignorance
and craving, and that neither the units into which we divide it,
i.e the "things" we believe to perceive, nor the connections we
postulate between them, have much validity. What are "atoms"
to the modern physicists, are the "dharmas" to the Buddhists. A
systematic classification of all dharmas had to wait for the
second period, just as in this matter of atoms a long time passed
between their initial conception by Demokritos and their more
precise study by Mendeleyev and Bohr. What we have in this
period are various numerical lists of dharmas — such as the five
"skandhas", i.e. form, feelings, perceptions, volitional impulses
and consciousness, which were said to constitute the whole
range of a human personality. Or the six external and internal
sense-fields, i.e. eye, ear, nose, tongue, touch-organ and mind,
as well as sight objects, sound-, smell-, taste-, touch- and mind-
objects, which constitute the whole range of our possible
experience. A "dharma" is an impersonal event, which belongs
to no person or individual, but just goes along on its own
objective way. It was regarded as a most praiseworthy achievement on the part of a Buddhist monk if he succeeded in

accounting to himself for the contents of his mind with the help of these impersonal dharmas, of which tradition provided him with definite lists, without ever bringing in the nebulous and pernicious word "I". No other religion has included anything like this in the mental training of its adherents and the originality of Buddhism is to be found largely in what it has to say about these elusive dharmas.

With regard to the *Samgha*, or "community", a visible and invisible Church are distinguished. The *visible* community consists first of all of the monks and nuns, and then in a wider sense it also comprises the laymen and laywomen who support the monks, have taken their refuge with the three Jewels, and promise to observe the five precepts. Within this community a small elite constituted the *true Samgha*. The wearing of the yellow robe merely shows that a man had exceptionally fine opportunities for spiritual attainment, but it does not render his spiritual success absolutely certain. As for the laymen, their status in the community was a most uncertain one, and for many of the monks they seemed to carry almost no weight at all. The true Samgha, the invisible Church, consisted of the Áryas, the "noble" or "holy" ones, men who were contrasted with the common worldlings, also known as the "foolish common people" (bála-prthag-janá).

The difference between these two classes of persons is fundamental to Buddhist theory. They are held to occupy two distinct planes of existence, respectively known as the "worldly" and the "supramundane".The saints alone are truly alive, while the worldlings just vegetate along in a sort of dull and aimless bewilderment. Not content with being born in the normal way, the saints have undergone a spiritual rebirth, which is technically known as "winning the Path". In other words, they have detached themselves from conditioned things to such an extent that they can now effectively turn to the Path which leads to Nirvana. The worldling's vision of Nirvana is obstructed by the things of the world which he takes far too seriously. Through prolonged meditation he can, however, reach a state where each time a worldly object rises up in front of him, he rejects it wholeheartedly as a mere hindrance, or nuisance. Once this aversion has become an ingrained habit, he can at last take Nirvana, the Unconditioned, for his object. Then "he ceases to belong to the common people", he "becomes one of the family of the Áryans". Thereafter he is less and less impelled by the motives of ordinary people, i.e. by motives which are a compound of self-interest and a misguided belief in the reality of sensory things and which contain a strong dosage of greed, hate, and delusion. The contrast with the vision of Nirvana reveals the insignificance and triviality of all these worldly concerns and Nirvana itself increasingly becomes the motivating force behind whatever is done.

Four kinds of saints are normally distinguished. The lowest is called a "Streamwinner", to indicate that he has won contact with the Path which leads to the Unconditioned. The saints are characteristically distinguished by the number of times they have to return to this world after death – the first kind must come back seven times at the most, the second only once, and the fourth, the Arhat, the finest and final product of this training, need never come back at all. The true Samgha is the community of all these saints, but the Arhats are those most highly prized.

4 THE SECTS AND THEIR DISPUTES

The Buddhist community did not remain united for long and soon fell apart into a number of sects. Indian Buddhist tradition

generally speaks of "eighteen" such sects, but that is a mere traditional number and in fact more than thirty are known to us,
at least by name. The Buddha appointed no successor and
Buddhism has never known a central authority like that of the
Pope or the Khalif. As different communities fixed themselves
in different parts of India, local traditions developed, though in
spite of all geographical and doctrinal divisions the different
sects generally speaking remained in constant communion with
each other. Not only did individual monks constantly travel
from one centre to another, but the institution of regular pil-
grimages of masses of monks and laymen to the holy places
of Magadha, which were hallowed by the life of the Buddha
and by the relics of His body, caused a constant intermin-
gling of the most diverse elements. The problems which the
sects discussed remained thus roughly the same for all and so
were the assumptions on which the solutions were based.
Through constant contact all Buddhists thus remained mutually
intelligible.

The different sects tended to have their own organization
and Scriptures. In many monasteries members of different sects
nevertheless lived together in perfect amity; it was generally recognized that the goal may be reached by different roads and the
sects showed great tolerance to each other, although occasional
sharp religious invective was of course not entirely unknown.
They all shared one common Dharma, although it is important
to realize that the verbal formulation of this Dharma did not
exist in a brief, handy and unambiguous form. It was transmitted
orally, to prevent it from reaching those unfit to receive it, but
there was so much of it that no one person could keep it all in
mind. In consequence different parts of the Scriptures were
handed to specialists who knew by heart, say, the Vinaya or the
Sútras, or a part of the Sútras, or the Abhidharma, and so on.

The reciters of each part of the Scriptures formed separate corporations with privileges of their own and their very existence would add to the divisions within the Order.

Nor must we forget that this Order, however much it might resent the fact, was not a self-contained entity, but had to co-exist with laymen on whom it was economically dependent. There was thus a constant tension between those who regarded the Dharma as a means for the production of a small elite of Arhats living in monastic seclusion in strict observance of the Vinaya rules, and those who wished to increase the chances of salvation for the ordinary people, while combating the authority of the Arhats and working for a relaxation of the monastic precepts.

Finally we must mention philosophy as one of the most potent causes of sectarian divisions. It is not difficult to see why philosophy should have played a decisive role in the development of Buddhism. Salvation on its higher levels was made dependent on the meditational awareness of the actual facts governing our mental processes. In the course of carrying out these meditations, the monks came up against problems which everywhere form the field of philosophy, such as the nature and classification of knowledge, the problems of causality, of time and space, of the criteria of reality, of the existence or non-existence of a "self" and so on. Now it is a fact of observation that philosophy differs from all other branches of knowledge in that it allows of more than one solution to each problem. It is in the nature of things that the differences of opinion should have multiplied the more the Buddhists went into the philosophical implications of their doctrine.

It would be clearly impossible here to enumerate the literally hundreds of points of dispute among the Buddhists, or even to give an account of all the sects. It will be sufficient to say a few words about the four or five chief sects, and leave the sub-sects to look after themselves. The following diagram shows the affiliations between the main branches of the Order:

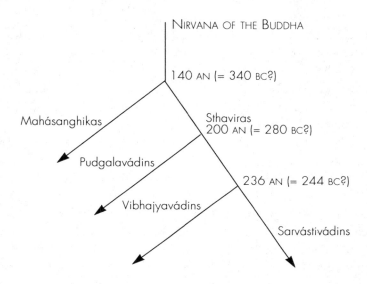

NIRVANA OF THE BUDDHA

140 AN (= 340 BC?)

Mahásanghikas

Sthaviras
200 AN (= 280 BC?)

Pudgalavádins

236 AN (= 244 BC?)

Vibhajyavádins

Sarvástivádins

The first schism, between *Mahásanghikas* and *Sthaviras*, was occasioned by the question of the status of the Arhats. A teacher by the name of Mahádeva arose, who claimed that in five points the Arhats fell short of the god-like stature which some sections of the community attributed to them. They could, among other things, have seminal emissions in their sleep, and that fact, so he argued, indicated that they are still subject to the influence of demonic deities who appear to them in their dreams. They are also still subject to doubts, ignorant of many things, and owe their salvation to the guidance of others. His thesis led to a dispute in which the majority took the side of Mahádeva, whose school in consequence called

themselves the Mahásanghikas. His adversaries took the name
of Sthaviras, "the Elders", claiming greater seniority and
orthodoxy. The Mahásanghikas continued to exist in India until
the end and important doctrinal developments took place
within their midst. All these were ultimately determined by
their decision to take the side of the people against the saints,
thus becoming the channel through which popular aspirations
entered into Buddhism.

Their most important theories concern Buddhology and
philosophical theory. As for the *Buddha*, they regarded everything personal, earthly, temporal and historical as outside the
real Buddha, Who was transcendental, altogether supramundane, had no imperfections and impurities whatsoever, was
omniscient, all-powerful, infinite and eternal, forever
withdrawn into trance, never distracted or asleep. In this way
the Buddha became an ideal object of religious faith. As for the
historical Buddha, He was a magical creation of the transcendental Buddha, a fictitious creature sent by Him to appear in
the world and to teach its inhabitants. While on the one side
intent on glorifying the otherworldliness of the Buddha, the
Mahásanghikas at the same time tried to increase the range of
His usefulness to ordinary people. The Buddha has not disap-
peared into Nirvana, but with a compassion as unlimited as the
length of His life, He will until the end of time conjure up all
kinds of messengers who will help all kinds of beings in diverse
ways. His influence is not confined to those few who can
understand His abstruse doctrines. As a Bodhisattva, i.e. during
the very long period which precedes His Buddhahood, He is
even reborn in the "states of woe", becomes of His own free
will an animal, a ghost or a dweller in hell and in many ways
furthers the weal of those beings who live in conditions in
which wisdom teaching must fall on deaf ears. Nor are Buddhas

found on this earth alone, but they fill the entire universe, and exist here and there everywhere, in all the world systems.

Two of the *philosophical theories of the Mahásanghikas* are of outstanding importance:

1. They taught that thought, in its own nature, its own being, in its substance, is perfectly pure and translucent. The impurities are accidental to it, never enter into or affect its original purity, and remain "adventitious" to it.

2. The Mahásanghikas were in the course of time led to an increasing scepticism about the value of verbalized and conceptualized knowledge. Some of them taught that all worldly things are unreal, because a result of the perverted views. Only that which transcends worldly things and can be called "emptiness", being the absence of all of them, is real. Others said that everything, both worldly and supramundane, both absolute and relative, both Samsára and Nirvana, is fictitious and unreal and that all we have got is a number of verbal expressions to which nothing real corresponds. In this way the Mahásanghikas early implanted the seeds which came to fruition in Maháyána Buddhism in the second period.

The second split, between the *Pudgalavádins* and the *Sthaviras*, concerned the question of pudgala, or "person". At the beginning of their history the "Personalists" were called *Vatsíputríyas*, after their founder, whereas later on they were better known as the *Sammitíyas*. Although barely orthodox they were at times strong in numbers, as we can see from the fact that Yüan Tsang in the seventh century counted 66,000 Personalist monks, out of a total of 250,000 in the whole of India. It was a fundamental dogma of Buddhist philosophy that personality is a token of falsehood and that no idea of "self", in whichever form it might appear, ought to have a place in the conception of reality as it actually is. The Personalists challenged this position and claimed that in addition to the impersonal dharmas there is still a Person to be reckoned with. They could adduce much scriptural authority in favour of their views. They were, for instance, fond of quoting the remark: "One person, when He is born in the world, is born for the weal of the many. Who is that one person? He is the Tathágata." Their opponents had to admit these and many other passages, but they maintained that they do not mean what they say, since in them the Buddha only conformed to the linguistic usage of an ignorant world.

The Personalists on the other hand taught that the Person is a reality in the ultimate sense, which provides a common factor or link for the successive processes occurring in a self-identical individual, over many lives, up to Buddhahood. At the same time the Pudgalavádins took great care to define the relation of the Person to the skandhas in such a way as not to contradict the essential principles of the Buddha's teaching and so as to exclude the "erroneous belief in a self". "The Person is neither identical with the skandhas, nor is he in the skandhas, nor outside them", so they taught. He provides, as we would put it, a kind of "structural unity" for the psycho-physical elements. As such he is "ineffable", indefinable in every respect whatsoever. A man's true, transcendental Self is indeed so subtle that only the Buddhas can see it. The Pudgalavádins represented the reaction of common-sense against the improbabilities of the dharmas-theory in its more uncompromising forms. They provided over the centuries a constant irritant to disputants of other sects and in some ways they were the forerunners of Maháyána philosophy. There exists a close analogy between the *pudgala* and the Suchness, or Emptiness, of the Mádhyamikas, and the "Store-consciousness" of the Yogácárins had many of the functions which the Personalists assigned to the *pudgala*.

Thirdly, the split between *Sarvástivádins* and *Vibhajyavádins* was occasioned by the pan-realistic ontological doctrine of Kátyáyaníputra, who taught that not only the present, but also past and future events are real. It appears that Aśoka sided with the Vibhajyavádins and that in consequence the Sarvástivádins went North and converted Kashmir, which remained their centre for more than a thousand years. When we consider the basic practice of Buddhist meditation, it is not surprising that the problem of the existence of past and future events should have seemed so important. Among the unsatisfactory features of this world the pride of place belonged to impermanence and it was the task of the Yogin to impress its full extent on his mind so as to further his distaste for worldly things. In this connection he had to take an event, or dharma, and see its "rise and fall", i.e. how it "comes, becomes, goes". Now, once a monk had got used to contrasting the past with the present and future, he might well become curious to know whether only the present really exists, or also the past and future. If only the present exists, this raises the further point of its duration, which many regarded as lasting just one single instant. In that case no thing will endure for any length of time, and one must assume that it is annihilated and re-created from instant to instant. This raises difficulties not only for the commonsense, but according to Kátyáyaníputra, also for the Buddhist doctrine of karma and retribution. For if a past action, which has ceased to exist immediately after taking place should lead to a reward or punishment many years later, then in that case something which does not exist is operative, has an effect, at a time when it does not exist. Likewise, so Kátyáyaníputra thought, the knowledge of past and future objects, as attested by memory and prediction, would be impossible, since no knowledge is possible without an actual object in front of the mind. In consequence he evolved the pan-realistic theory, which became the peculiar thesis of the Sarvástivádins. It avoided the difficulties mentioned above only to introduce many others in their stead and a vast superstructure of auxiliary hypotheses was required to make it tenable. In spite of their addiction to a rather tortuous scholasticism, the Sarvástivádins became the most significant school on the Indian subcontinent.

As the result of the emergence of an interest in philosophical questions we have the first instance of a whole class of canonical literature being created to meet a new situation. The *Abhidharma* books were clearly composed after the third division of the schools. The contents of the seven Abhidharma books of the Sarvástivádins differ greatly from those of the seven books of the Theravádins, who are an offshoot of the Vibhajyavádins. Some sects, like the Sautrántikas, went so far as to contest the authenticity of all Abhidharma works. A great mental effort went, from about 200 BC onwards, into the production of these books, which are technical handbooks of meditation, teaching what events can be regarded as elementary, how others are composed of them, how they condition each other, etc.

Before we leave the schools, we may mention a few more points of disagreement on questions of a more general interest. The elusive concept of Nirvana came in for some discussion. If it is unconditioned, does it exist, and can it have effects? Is it the only unconditioned thing, or is space also unconditioned? Is there any difference between the Nirvana of the Buddhas and that of other people, and what is it? There was also much interest in determining the criteria of a *definite achievement*, which cannot again be lost. There was therefore much debate on when and whether the Arhats and other saints can "fall back" and from when onwards their salvation is assured. On the subject of *death*, always present in the minds of these ascetics, one wondered whether the hour of death is definitely fixed by karma, or whether a premature and untimely death is possible. There was also disagreement on what follows on death: five schools believed that death is instantly followed by rebirth in another organism, whereas five other schools taught that death would be followed by an "intermediary existence" of up to forty-nine days, during which in most cases the new incarnation slowly prepared itself. In the case of certain saints this interval is used for the attainment of the Nirvana which escaped them during this life.

5 THE LAITY

We have now sketched the basic opinions and aims of the homeless monks who constitute the essential core of the Buddhist world. But what about those Buddhists who were not monks, what about the laity without whom the monks could not possibly carry on their meditations? What is their place in the scheme of things? What are they given to do? And what do the monks do for them?

If a layman feels tied to his home and unable to escape from it into the homeless life, it is due to his deficiency in a quality called "merit", which depends on what he has done in the past and which circumscribes his access to spiritual opportunities. A number of exceptional cases are recorded of laymen having won deathlessness without previously entering the Order. Generally speaking, however, their salvation is out of the question at present, and can be assured only on condition that by a future life they have accumulated sufficient "merit" to make the jump into the social freedom of the monastic life. The layman's one and only religious task at present can be to increase his store of merit. The Buddhist religion offers him four avenues for doing so:

1. He must observe the five precepts (see p. 16), or at least some of them. On feast days, every fortnight, he may add to them another three, i.e. he fasts, avoids worldly amusements, and uses neither unguents nor ornaments. A few observed still two more precepts, i.e. they did not sleep on a high, big bed and they accepted no gold or silver.

2. He must have devotion for the Three Treasures (see p. 18) and faith is the virtue apposite to a householder's state of life. But this faith is not an exclusive one and does not entail a rejection of his ancestral beliefs and of the Brahmanic religious usages of his social environment. The Triple Jewel is not a jealous God and is not displeased by the worship of the deities of a man's country or caste.

3. He must be generous, especially to the monks, and give as much as possible to them, not only for their upkeep, but also for religious buildings inhabited by no one. To some extent the merit produced by gifts depends on the spiritual endowments of the recipient, and therefore the sons of Śākyamuni, and in particular the Arhats, are the best possible "field for planting merit".

4. He may worship the relics of the Buddha (see p. 21). The actual attitude of the Buddhists to these teeth and bones is difficult to describe in terms readily understood in the West. It is obviously impossible for them to "pray" to the Buddha, for the reason that He is no longer there, being in Nirvana, i.e. extinct as far as this world is concerned. It is even doubtful whether the word "worship" is a very suitable one. Before the advent of modern industrialism men everywhere looked upon the world as a mysterious realm of boundless possibilities, full of invisible forces, meaningful and replete with significant hints. The posture of namaskára, in which the folded extended palms are held forth, is the customary mode of greeting in India. Bigotry, servility and

superstitious idolatry do not enter into it. All these things rest very lightly on the true believer and do not constrain his inner freedom. The fervour of the faithful filled the Buddhist world with innumerable shrines (caitya) and Stúpas, which became the object of the special devotion of householders. The creation and cult of Buddha images is, however, fairly late, and unlikely to go back before the first century AD.

If a layman well observes these four duties, he will be happy in this life, and after his death he will be reborn in heaven, or in paradise. The Emperor Aśoka well exemplifies the character of Buddhism as understood by the laity. Among Buddhist doctrines he regarded as the two most important ones the avoiding of doing harm to others (ahimsá) and the active benevolence towards them (maitrí). His edicts contain many moral exhortations to the practice of the simple virtues and we also hear much about the need for piety. But there is nothing in them about the deeper ideas or fundamental tenets of the faith. There is no mention of the four holy Truths, the eightfold path, the chain of causation, or even of Nirvana, or of the supernatural qualities of a Buddha.

What benefits then does the monk bestow upon the laymen? He increases both their spiritual and their material welfare. He promotes the first by sermons on those aspects of the doctrine which are intelligible and relevant to the laity, as well as by the example of a holy life which will give courage and zest to those still tied to the world and can give them a glimpse of the freedom and serenity they may achieve in a future life. In the course of time a vast literature of Birth stories (játaka), which tell of the Buddha's previous lives, animal as well as human, and of edifying tales (avadána) was composed for the benefit of the laity. These stories were listened to with avidity, but they had less authority than the more metaphysical teachings. Their message concerns chiefly the virtues of secular life. They constantly stress the doctrine of karma and rebirth and also foster a tenderness towards all that lives. In Bharhut, Bodhgaya, Sanchi, Nagarjunikonda and Ajanta many of the Játaka tales have been illustrated in sculpture and painting.

It was also a belief of Buddhist Asia that the material well-being of the people, their economic prosperity and their freedom from famine, epidemics and wars, was largely the work of the monks. For the welfare of a nation depends chiefly on the benevolence of occult and spiritual forces, which the monks alone can know about and which they alone can propitiate. All is well with a people which respects the monks, showing its reverence for the Buddhas by generous gifts to the monasteries and for temples and shrines, but a nation which turns its back on the religion is doomed to perish in misery. These were the beliefs which helped to maintain the monastic institutions.

The voluntary and sporadic support of a population tied to them by links as tenuous as these would, however, not have kept the Order going for long. The secret behind its social survival over the centuries lay in the ability of the Buddhists, repeated over and over again, to enlist the support of Asian rulers, who maintained the monastic institutions out of government funds. In default of this, the monks were driven to become large property owners in their own right and to dispense altogether with the capricious rewards of begging from house to house. This is also a solution, but it imperils aloofness from the things of this world and is apt to draw the monks back into the arena of social strife.

Nevertheless relations with the laity were always precarious and there at its base was the Achilles heel of the whole soaring edifice. If Buddhism departed from the tenets of the first period, it was largely the work of the laity. It was their pressure which did much to bring about the reforms of the second and third period, reforms which therefore appeared to the strict monastic party as a degeneration. The Maháyána gave much greater weight to the laymen. It could count on much popular support for its opinion that people are as important as dharmas, for its attacks on the selfishness of monks who think only of their own welfare, for its constant censure of "haughty" and "conceited" monks and for its stories of wealthy householders, such as Vimalakírti, who surpassed the oldest and most venerable monks in the splendour of their spiritual attainments. The same kind of popular pressure would induce the monks to become more manifestly useful to laymen. In the third, Tantric, period they inserted themselves into their magical beliefs and acted as astrologers, exorcisers, weather makers, doctors, etc. That is why the story of Buddhism becomes unintelligible unless due weight is given to the desires of the dumb common people. The stone which the builders had rejected became the cornerstone after all.

6 EXPANSION

During this period, Buddhism remained on the whole a purely Indian religion. The emperor Aśoka, about 250 BC, sent some missions to the successors of Alexander the Great, i.e. to the Greek kingdoms of the diadochs in Egypt, Macedon, Cyrene and Epirus. These missions have left no trace and they may very well have been ineffective. The rather dim awareness of Buddhism which we find in Greek authors can be accounted for by later contacts which took place in connection with the trade which flourished in Roman times between India and the Mediterranean.

It was only in Ceylon that Aśoka's missionary activity bore fruit. Once brought there about 240 BC by Mahinda, Aśoka's son, Buddhism has existed in Ceylon for a longer stretch of time than anywhere else. From that time onwards Buddhism has been the state religion of Ceylon. Only Buddhists had a legitimate right to be kings and the island of Lanká was held to belong to the Buddha Himself. It was the king's duty to protect the Order of monks and great benefits accrued to the monasteries in the form of donations, prestige and protection from interference. The kings, although mostly laymen, were also the final judges in any dispute which might arise among the Buddhists. The monks in their turn generally helped the kings and won popular support for their wishes. This close connection of the Samgha with the state had its disadvantages. From the second century BC onwards it not only infused a spirit of nationalism into the Buddhism of Ceylon and made the monks prone to political intrigue, but it also led them to enthusiastically support the national wars of their kings. They assured king Dutta Gámaní (101–77 BC) that the killing of many thousands of enemies was of no account, because as unbelievers they were really no more than animals. They accompanied the army of the same king, "since the sight of bhikkhus is both blessing and protection for us", and the king himself had a relic of the Buddha put into his spear.

For a long time Ceylonese Buddhists continued to be in lively contact with India over the ports of Bharukaccha and Súrpáraka in the West. Gradually the whole Canon came to Ceylon and towards the end of our period, or even later, also new works composed in Páli in India by the mother-sect, such as the first part of the "Questions of King Milinda" and the "Niddesa". During the first century BC the Canon and Commentaries, so far transmitted orally, were written down at

Aluvihára, "so that the Dharma might endure". War and famine had depopulated the country and the oral transmission of the Pitakas was in danger. The holy language of the Canon was Páli, whereas the Commentaries were in Sinhalese. Ceylon became the home of a school known as the Theravádins – of great interest in the history of Buddhism partly because their Canon is preserved in its entirety and partly because in their geographical isolation they remained relatively unaffected by many of the later developments. It is not, however, very clear what Continental school they were derived from. Probably they were akin to the Indian Vibhajyavádins, and an offshoot of one of their branches.

CHAPTER

2

THE
SECOND PERIOD
AD 0–500

1 THE MAHÁYÁNA IN INDIA

About the beginning of the Christian era a new trend took shape in Buddhism, known as the Maháyána, literally "the great vehicle". It was prepared by the exhaustion of the old impulse which produced fewer and fewer Arhats, by the tensions within the doctrines as they had developed by then and by the demands of the laity for more equal rights with the monks. Foreign influences also had a great deal to do with it. The Maháyána developed in North-West India and South India, the two regions where Buddhism was most exposed to non-Indian influences, to the impact of Greek art in its Hellenistic and Romanized forms and to the influence of ideas from both the Mediterranean and the Iranian world. This cross-fertilization incidentally rendered the Buddhism of the Maháyána fit for export outside India. So that it should be able to travel outside India, Buddhism had first to be somewhat modified by foreign influences, had to undergo a preliminary phase of de-Indianization. Before it could be received by alien cultures it had first to receive an impression from them. Roughly speaking only in its modified Maháyána form has it been able to live outside India. In due course the Maháyána has conquered the entire northern half of the Buddhist world, and the Buddhists of Nepal, Tibet, Mongolia, China, Korea and Japan are nearly all Maháyánists.

The Mahāyāna developed in two stages: first in an unsystematic form, which went on between 100 BC and AD 500, and then, after AD 150, in a systematized philosophical form, which led to two distinct schools, the Mādhyamikas and the Yogācārins.

We must first of all explain the main features of the *early Mahāyāna*. About 100 BC a number of Buddhists felt that the existing statements of the doctrine had become stale and useless. In the conviction that the Dharma requires ever new re-formulations so as to meet the needs of new ages, new populations and new social circumstances, they set out to produce a new literature. The creation of this literature is one of the most magnificent outbursts of creative energy known to human history and it was sustained for about four to five centuries. Repetition alone, they believed, cannot sustain a living religion. Unless counterbalanced by constant innovation, it will become fossilized and lose its life-giving qualities.

So far the Mahāyānistic attitude seems quite logical. What is more difficult to understand is that they insisted in presenting these new writings, manifestly composed centuries after the Buddha's death, as the very words of the Buddha Himself. In order to make room for the new dispensation, they followed the Mahāsanghikas in minimizing the importance of the historical Buddha Śākyamuni, whom they replaced by the Buddha who is the embodiment of Dharma (*dharmakāya*). In the "Lotus of the Good Law" we are told that the Buddha, far from having reached His enlightenment at Bodhgāya, about 500 BC or whenever the date may have been, abides for aeons and aeons, from eternity to eternity, and that He preaches the Law at all times in countless places and innumerable disguises. In the "Diamond Sūtra" occurs the famous verse:

Those who by my form did see me,
And those who followed me by voice,
Wrong the efforts they engaged in,
Me those people will not see!
From the Dharma-body should one see the Buddhas,
From the Dharma-bodies comes their guidance.

The conception of the Buddha as the timeless embodiment of all Truth allowed for a successive revelation of that truth by Him at different times. Not content with this, the Maháyánists tried to link their own new writings with the historical Buddha by a number of mythological fictions. They asserted that they had been preached by the Buddha in the course of His life on earth, that parallel to the Council at Rájagrha, which codified the Sútras of the Hínayána, the Maháyána Sútras had been codified by an assembly of Bodhisattvas on the mythical mountain of Vimalasvabháva; that the texts had been miraculously preserved for five centuries and stored away in the subterranean palaces of the Nágas, or with the king of the Gandharvas, or the king of the Gods. Then, as Nágárjuna puts it, "five hundred years after the Buddha's Nirvana, when the Good Law, after having gradually declined, was in great danger", these treasures from the past were unearthed, revealed and made known, so as to revivify the doctrine.

What then were the main doctrinal innovations of the Maháyána? They can be summarized under five headings:

1. As concerns the goal there is a shift from the Arhat-ideal to the Bodhisattva-ideal;
2. A new way of salvation is worked out, in which compassion ranks equal with wisdom, and which is marked by the

gradual advance through six "perfections" (páramitá);

3. Faith is given a new range by being provided with a new pantheon of deities, or rather of persons more than divine;

4. "Skill in means" (upáyakauśalya), an entirely new virtue, becomes essential to the saint, and is placed even above wisdom, the highest virtue so far;

5. A coherent ontological doctrine is worked out, dealing with such items as "Emptiness", "Suchness", etc.

We will now consider these five points one by one.

1. The goal of Arhatship, which had motivated Buddhism in the first period, is now relegated to the second place. The Maháyánistic saint strives to be a "Bodhisattva" – from bodhi, "enlightenment", and sattva, "being" or "essence". A Bodhisattva is distinguished by three features: (a) In his essential being he is actuated by the desire to win the full enlightenment of a Buddha, which, from this point of view, implies complete omniscience, i.e. the knowledge of all things at all times in all their details and aspects. (b) He is dominated by two forces, in equal proportion, i.e. by compassion and wisdom. From compassion he selflessly postpones his entrance into the bliss of Nirvana so as to help suffering creatures. From wisdom he attempts to win insight into the emptiness of all that is. He persists in his compassionate solidarity with all that lives although his wisdom shows him that living beings and all their woes are purely illusory. (c) Although intent on ultimate purity, a Bodhisattva remains in touch with ordinary people in having the same passions they have. His passions, however, do not either affect or pollute his mind.

2. A Bodhisattva's compassion is called "great", because it is boundless and makes no distinctions. A Bodhisattva resolves to become the saviour of all, whatever may be their worth or their

claim to his attention. In the first period the wisdom of the saints had been fully emphasized, but now their selfless desire to make others happy is said to rank equal in value with it. Enlightenment is the thorough and complete understanding of the nature and meaning of life, the forces which shape it, the method to end it, and the reality which lies beyond it. This enlightenment, the Mahásánists agreed, does not automatically entail the desire to assist others. Among the enlightened they distinguished three types, two of them "selfish", one "unselfish". The "selfish" types are the Arhats and Pratyekabuddhas, who are said to represent the idea of the Hínayána, of the "inferior vehicle". They are described as aloof from the concerns of the world and intent on their own private salvation alone. The "unselfish" ones are the Buddhas, and the pursuit of the unselfish quest for enlightenment on the part of a Bodhisattva is called the "Buddha-vehicle", of the "Great Vehicle" (mahá-yána).

A Bodhisattva must be a patient man. He wants to become a Buddha, but his distance from the transcendental perfection of a supreme Buddha, Who both knows and is everything, will obviously be nearly infinite. In one life it could not possibly be traversed. Countless lives would be needed and a Bodhisattva must be prepared to wait for aeons and aeons before he can reach his goal. Yet, he is separated from Buddhahood only by one single small obstacle, i.e. his belief in a personal self, his assumption that he is a separate Individual, his inveterate tendency towards "I-making and Mine-making" (*ahamkárama-makára*). To get rid of himself is the Bodhisattva's supreme task. By two kinds of measures he tries to remove himself from himself – actively by self-sacrifice and selfless service, cogni-tively by insight into the objective non-existence of a self. The first is due to his compassion, the second to wisdom, defined as the ability to penetrate to the true reality, to the "own-being" of things, to what they are in and by themselves. It is believed that action and cognition must always go hand in hand to bring forth their spiritual fruits.

The unity of compassion and wisdom is acted out by the six "perfections", or *páramitá*, the six "methods by which we go to the Beyond". A person turns into a Bodhisattva when he first resolves to win full enlightenment for the benefit of all beings. Thereafter, until his attainment of Buddhahood, aeons and aeons are devoted to the practice of the Páramitás. So important is this concept that the Maháyána often refers to itself as the "Vehicle of the Páramitás". The six are: the perfections of giving, morality, patience, vigour, meditation and wisdom. The first enjoins generosity, a willingness to give away all that one has, even one's own body, and the second the scrupulous observance of the moral precepts, even at the risk of one's own life. As for "patience", the Maháyána has much more to say about it than the Hínayána and it uses the word in a wider sense than is usual. As a moral virtue it means the patient endurance of all kinds of suffering and hostility and the absence of any feeling of anger or discontent when meeting with them. In addition, "patience" is here also considered as an intellectual virtue and as such it means the emotional acceptance, before one has fathomed the whole of their depth, of the more incredible and anxiety-producing ontological doctrines of the Maháyána, such as the non-existence of all things. Vigour means that the Bodhisattva indefatigably persists in his work over the ages and never feels discouraged; his perfection of meditation enables him to gain proficiency in trances "numerous as the sands of the Ganges". The perfection of wisdom finally is the ability to understand the essential properties of all processes and phenomena, their mutual relations, the conditions which bring about their rise and fall, and the ultimate unreality of their separate existence. At its highest point it leads right into the Emptiness which is the one and only reality.

3. Another distinctive contribution of the Maháyána is the distinction of ten stages which the Bodhisattva must traverse on his way to Buddhahood. This aspect of the doctrine reached its final formulation in the third century in the "Sútra on the Ten Stages". The first six of these stages correspond to the six "perfections" and each of them is marked by the intensive practice of one of them. The sixth stage therefore corresponds to the perfection of wisdom and with it the Bodhisattva has by his understanding of emptiness come "face to face" (*abhimukhí*) with Reality itself. At that point he would be able to escape from the terrors of this world of birth-and-death and he could, if he wanted to, enter into Nirvana. Out of compassion he nevertheless makes no use of this possibility, but stays on in the world for a long time so as to help those in it. Although in the world, he now is no longer of it. During the last four stages a Bodhisattva gains what the texts call "sovereignty over the world", and he becomes a kind of supernatural being endowed with miraculous powers of many kinds. From the ordinary Bodhisattvas as they exist on the first six stages, the "celestial Bodhisattvas" of the last four stages differ in that they were well suited to becoming objects of a religious cult. Soon the faithful increasingly turned to all kinds of mythical Bodhisattvas, such as Avalokiteśvara, Mañjuśrí, Maitreya, Kshítigarbha, Samantabhadra and others. Though conceived in India some of these Bodhisattvas show strong non-Indian, and particularly Iranian, influences.

The development of mythical Bodhisattvas was accompanied, and even preceded by, that of mythical Buddhas, who were held to reside in the heavens in all the ten directions. In the East lives Akshobhya, the "Imperturbable". In the West is the kingdom of the Buddha of "Infinite Light", Amitábha, not always clearly distinguished from Amitáyus, the Buddha who "has an infinite life-span". Amitáyus is a counterpart to the Iranian Zurvan Akaranak ("Unlimited Time"), just as the cult of Amitábha owed much to Iranian sun worship and probably originated in the Kushana Empire in the borderland between India and Iran. There are many other celestial Buddhas, in fact infinitely many, and most of them have a "kingdom" of their own, a world which is not of this world, a land which is "pure" because free from defilements and adverse conditions.

4. Next we must say a few words about the "skill in means", a virtue which is indispensable to a Bodhisattva at all times, but which he possesses in its fullness only late, on the seventh stage, after the "perfection of wisdom" has thoroughly shown him the emptiness of everything that seems to be. "Skill in means" is the ability to bring out the spiritual potentialities of different people, by statements or actions which are adjusted to their needs and adapted to their capacity for comprehension. If the truth be told, all that we have described so far as constituting the doctrine of the Maháyána is just "skill in means" and nothing more. It is a series of fictions elaborated to further the salvation of beings. In actual fact there are no Buddhas, no Bodhisattvas, no perfections, and no stages. All these are products of our imagination, just expedients, concessions to the needs of ignorant people, designed to ferry them across to the Beyond. Everything apart from the One, also called "Emptiness" or "Suchness", is devoid of real existence, and whatever may be said about it is ultimately untrue, false and nugatory. But nevertheless it is not only permissible, but even useful to say it, because the salvation of beings demands it.

5. So far we have spoken about the way to the Beyond. Now we come to the Beyond itself. Wisdom teachings about ontology, or the nature of reality, constitute the inner core of the Maháyána doctrine. These teachings are extremely subtle, abstruse and elusive and defy any attempt at summarizing them, because they are not meant as definite statements about definite facts and because it is said expressly that they do not explain anything, do not say anything in particular, for the ultimate transcendental reality is held to lie beyond the grasp of intellectual comprehension and verbal expression. Be that as it may, the peculiar ontological doctrines of the Maháyána developed logically from the philosophy of the Mahásanghikas and in direct and conscious opposition to that of the Sarvástivádins. Four basic propositions are common to all Maháyánists:

1. All dharmas are "empty" in the sense that each one is nothing in and by itself. Any dharma is therefore indistinguishable from any other dharma. In consequence all dharmas are ultimately non-existent and the same.
2. This Emptiness can be called "Suchness", when one takes each thing "such as it is", without adding anything to it or subtracting anything from it. There can be only one Suchness and the multiple world is a construction of our imagination.
3. If all is one and the same, then also the Absolute will be identical with the Relative, the Unconditioned with the conditioned, Nirvana with Samsára.
4. True Knowledge must rise above the duality of either subject and object, or of affirmation and negation.

These four propositions get near to the Beyond, but they do not quite reach it. The inmost sanctum of the whole doctrine is filled with nothing but silence.

We now come to the *systematized Maháyána*, which falls into two main philosophical schools, the Mádhyamikas and the Yogácárins. The *Mádhyamika* school was founded by Nágárjuna (c AD 150), a South Indian and one of the greatest minds India has produced. The school persisted for many centuries and has had a vigorous life also in China and Tibet. The Mádhyamika philosophy is primarily a logical doctrine which aims at an all-embracing scepticism by showing that all statements are equally untenable. This applies also to statements about the Absolute. They are all bound to be false and the Buddha's "thundering silence" alone can do justice to it. Soteriologically, everything must be dropped and given up, until absolute Emptiness alone remains, and then salvation is gained.

At the time of Nágárjuna the shadowy beginnings of *Yogácárin* thinking could already be discerned, but the philosophy itself was clearly formulated only in the fourth century. Vasubandhu and Asanga are the greatest names here and modern historical research has so far not succeeded in sorting out the many conflicting data we have on their chronology, writings and activities. The Yogácárins propounded a primarily psychological theory and believed that the Absolute can usefully be described as "Mind", "Thought" or "Consciousness".

Theirs was a metaphysical idealism, according to which consciousness creates its objects out of its own inner potentialities. Mind can, however, exist quite by itself, without any object whatever. Soteriologically, the Yogácárins aimed at achieving "an act of cognition which no longer apprehends an object". Salvation is won when we can produce in ourselves an act of thought which is "Thought-only", pure consciousness, and altogether beyond the division between subject and object.

The two systems were clearly quite distinct in their interests and intentions. The polemics which they occasionally directed against each other had therefore little effect and occupy little space in their writings. On the whole each school was content to elaborate its own tenets, without paying too much attention to its rivals. To the Mádhyamikas, the Yogácárin doctrine appeared as a quite incomprehensible perversity, whereas the Yogácárins regarded the Mádhyamika doctrine as a preliminary stage of their own, which however missed the true and esoteric core of the Buddha's teaching.

The Yogácárin school is further noteworthy for having elaborated the final formulation of the doctrine of the *three Bodies of the Buddha*. The Buddha is said to exist on three distinct levels. As the Dharma-body He is the Absolute, Truth and Reality itself. In His "communal body", or His "enjoyment body" (*sámbhoga-káya*), the Buddha shows Himself to the celestial Bodhisattvas and other superhuman beings and preaches in unearthly realms the Dharma to them, generating joy, delight and love for it. Finally there is the fictitious, or conjured up body (*nirmána-káya*), which is the one that human beings see appearing at certain times on earth and which is a phantom body sent by the real Buddha to do His work in the world. By way of scholastic refinement, many Yogácárins still added a fourth Body, the Substantial Body (*svábhávika-káya*), which is the basis of the other three.

Yet a note of caution must here be sounded. It is generally said that this doctrine of the Three Bodies was first formulated by the Yogácárins about AD 300, but basically there is nothing really new about it. All three bodies had been known centuries before. The identification of one side of the Buddha with the Dharma had often been made in the first period and is of the essence of Buddhism. As to the second body, there had been a long-standing tradition about the "thirty-two marks of the superman" (see p. 21), which were obviously not attributes of the body visible to all, but adhered to some glorified body which is visible only to the eyes of faith and manifests itself only to the community of the saints. Although the assumption of such a "glorified" body had been made for a long time, all references to it until about AD 300 are vague and elusive. It may be that the doctrine on this subject was not fully developed before the third century. It may also be, however, that this was regarded as a particularly sacred, and therefore secret, subject, which could be explained only orally to those who were spiritually qualified to hear of it, while the remainder had to content themselves with a few vague hints. It is likely that the continuous decline of which we spoke before (p. 5) was accompanied by an increasing profanization of the doctrine. In early times, as we saw (p. 12), a monk was even forbidden to recite the actual text of the Sútras to laymen. We hear of Anáthapindada, one of the greatest early benefactors of the Order, that only on his death-bed, after having for many years honoured the Lord and helped the Samgha, he was allowed to hear from Sáriputra a sermon on the unsatisfactory nature of sense-objects, because, as Sáriputra told him, such subjects were reserved for the yellow-robed monks and were not normally taught to the men in white robes, to the laymen. Later on, first the Sútras ceased to be secret and further on also the more secret teachings hidden behind them were divulged one by one. As a matter of fact the Yogácárins always claimed that all they did was to explain the "esoteric" meaning, known all along, but never broadcast to all and sundry.

If this is so, then what in the history of Buddhist thought seems to be doctrinal innovation may very often be nothing but the gradual shifting of the line between esoteric and exoteric teachings. At first, even up to Aśoka, the bulk of the doctrine, except for some moral maxims and so on, was esoteric. By the time of the Tantra, in the third period, even the most esoteric doctrines were written down. This process can be understood as one of compensation for the increasing admitted failure to achieve the spiritual goals aimed at. The monks who were unable to succeed inwardly in their self-realization would then indulge in the extroverted activity of spreading their doctrines among the general population. From the fact that a statement is attested only at a later date we cannot therefore conclude with any cogency that it was actually invented at that time. It is just as possible that it ceased at that time to be the prerogative of the initiated and became more or less public property.

2 HÍNAYÁNA DEVELOPMENTS IN INDIA

In spite of the growth of the Maháyána, the old Hínayána schools held their own. The new developments naturally had some influence on them. They adopted some Maháyána theories, either by direct borrowing or because they were exposed to the same influences which shaped the Maháyána. The idea of a Bodhisattva now becomes prominent in the vast popular Játaka literature which tells stories about the Buddha's former lives. Originally these tales were fables, fairy-tales, anecdotes, etc., taken from the vast fund of Indian folklore. These current tales were then adapted to Buddhist uses by being represented as incidents in the lives of the historical Buddha. For a long time they were just told to illustrate the glory and spiritual stature of the Lord (*Bhagavan*). Only at a later age were they recast into the form of stories about the Bodhisattva. In connection with the Játakas a set of ten "perfections" was elaborated, parallel to the six perfections of the Maháyána. Also the compassion and the loving-kindness, which in older literature is a minor and very subordinate virtue, becomes more prominent in these tales of the Bodhisattva's deeds, the "Bodhisattva" always being the Buddha in His previous lives. Likewise the doctrine of "emptiness" is now stressed more than it was in the past. A recognition of the fact that the times are bad and the days for the Arhats have passed, gives greater respectability to the aspiration after the secondary goals, such as the rebirth among the gods, or with Maitreya, the future Buddha, now in the Tushita heaven. But on the whole these concessions are made rather grudgingly. Our Hínayána sources practically never mention the Maháyánists, either positively or negatively. They were somewhat incredulous of all these innovations and they refused to take seriously the claim that the many new Maháyána works gave the Buddha's actual words. In fact they rejected these works as just so many "concoctions" and unworthy of serious consideration. The eloquent testimony of the complete and total silence of all Hínayána doctors on the subject of the Maháyána shows clearly what they thought of all this splendour.

Undeterred by the Maháyána, the Hínayánists went on with their own doctrinal development, which consisted in working out the logical implications of their Abhidharma. The elaboration and systematization of the Abhidharma occupied the first four centuries of our era. After that time it was completed for the two principal schools of which we have any precise knowledge, i.e. by Vasubandhu for the Sarvástivádins and by Buddhaghosa for the Theravádins. About AD 400 the Hínayánists reached the perfection of which they were capable. After that there was no more to come and the Indian Hínayána, although it persisted for another 800 years, has left us few records of further creative intellectual activity. Vasubandhu himself felt that he had reached the end of an epoch and he concludes his "Abhidharmakośa" with the famous words,

The times are come
When flooded by the rising tide of ignorance
Buddha's religion seems to breathe its last.

The creation of the Abhidharma was one of the greatest achievements of the human intellect. On pp. 22–3 I have explained to some extent the sense in which the word "dharmas" was used. In our second period one attempted to determine systematically how many kinds of "dharmas", or ultimate constituents of experience, had to be assumed. The Sarvástivádins arrived at a list of 75 dharmas, whereas the Theravádins believed that 174 were necessary. The difference between the two lists is much less serious than it appears to be. The Theravádin list is so much longer chiefly because they sub-divided one item of the Sarvástivádins (i.e. no. 14, Thought) into the 89 kinds of consciousness. Otherwise the lists mainly differ in their arrangement, order of enumeration and terminology, as well as in a number of trifling details too wearisome to enumerate here. The basic factors were already worked out while the two schools were still united and only the final touches were added at a later period.

The astounding range of Abhidharma studies can be appreciated when we look at the topics which Vasubandhu discusses in his *Abhidharmakośa*. It falls into eight chapters, dealing with the elements, the powers and faculties, cosmology, i.e. the origin, arrangement and destruction of the universe, with karma, the passions, the various kinds of saints and the paths which lead to salvation, concluding with a survey of sacred cognition and meditational attainments. In addition an appendix is devoted to the refutation of the views of Buddhists and non-Buddhists who postulate the existence of an ego, the abolition and eradication of all such views being Vasubandhu's main object in the composition of his treatise.

The final synthesis was preceded by many lengthy and extensive discussions of which we have for the Sarvástivádins some documents left. In the first century of our era they fixed their Canon, about AD 100 there is the *Vibháshá*, a commentary to the Abhidharma, and about AD 200 the enormous *Mahávibhásha*, a commentary to the *Jñánaprasthána* composed by 500 Arhats of Kashmir, which gives the name of *Vaibháshika* to the most orthodox school of the Sarvástivádins. The word vibháshá can be translated as "option" and the works just mentioned derived their name from the fact that different opinions of the leading teachers of the school are carefully recorded, so that the reader may be able to choose those which seem most likely to him. The chief adversaries of the Vaibháshikas were the Sautrántikas who did not believe that the seven basic Abhidharma texts had been preached by the Buddha, and regarded the statements on Abhidharma which are scattered in the Sútras as the only reliable scriptural basis for that subject. The doctrines of the Sautrántikas are often simpler and more obviously reasonable than those of the Sarvástivádins. The controversies between the two schools dealt with such subjects as the possibility of self-consciousness, or that of the direct perception of objects. Or one debated in what sense external objects really exist, or what it is that does the "seeing" (the eyes, or the consciousness, or mind), or whether destruction has a cause or comes about automatically of itself in the very nature of things. Vasubandhu made many concessions to the Sautrántika point of view, and his *Kośa* was in consequence assailed by the orthodox Vaibháshikas. He found an able and powerful opponent in Samghabhadra, who commented on the *Kośa* from the traditional point of view. Nevertheless the *Kośa* was increasingly recognized as the last word on the subject and numerous commentaries testify to its enduring popularity in subsequent centuries.

The creative activities of the Hínayána were, however, not entirely confined to the Abhidharma. Constant additions were made to the Birth Stories and Edifying Tales. The life and personality of the Buddha claimed the attention of the devotees. Aśvaghosa (c. 100), a very fine poet, used the devices of Indian Sanskrit poetics to popularize the life of the Buddha by his *Buddhacarita*, into which he introduced much Hindu learning. His work is marked by great devotional feeling, but there is no reason to assume that Aśvaghosa was a Maháyánist in any precise sense of the term and his views show more affinity to those of the Mahásanghikas than to any other known school. Aśvaghosa also wrote dramas, which have since his time been favourite means of popularizing Buddhist sentiments. In Burma and Tibet some of the longer Játakas, like the famous story of Vessantara, who gave away all he had, are still popular subjects of dramatic performances. In the fifth century a biography of the Buddha from the period aeons ago when he first decided to attain Buddhahood, down to the beginning of His teaching, was compiled in Ceylon, in the form of an introduction to the Pali Játaka book. We also have Mátrceta's (c. 150) "Hymn in 150 Verses", lauding "the Buddha's great and profound virtues", which was taught to all monks. Piety and not wisdom was the aim of this kind of literature.

3 NEPAL AND KASHMIR

In *Nepal* the religion seems to have existed for a long time, probably from the beginning of Buddhism onwards. Little is, however, known of the period before the seventh century AD, and the Buddhism of Nepal was in all probability not substantially different from that of Northern India. In the legendary history of the *Svayambhúpurána* a great role is assigned to Mañjuśrí, who came from China to Svayambhú, made the great lake disappear which up to then had filled the valley, founded the city of Kathmandu and placed there as a ruler the king

Dharmíkara whom he had brought with him from Mahá-Cína. The Buddha Himself was born in Nepal, at Lumbiní, and Aśoka is known to have visited His birthplace, where he erected an inscribed pillar.

Although probably known in *Kashmir* before Aśoka, Buddhism really made its influence felt only during his rule, when Kashmir formed part of his Empire. The *bhikshu* Madhyántika was sent to convert the country. Aśoka is said to have built 500 monasteries for the Arhats, and to have given the valley itself as a gift to the Samgha. Thereafter the fate of Buddhism fluctuated with the attitude of the rulers.

Under Kanishka a Council is said to have been held which fixed the Sarvástivádin Canon. From that time onwards the Sarvástivádin writings were normally in Sanskrit, and this fact by itself would increase the relative weight of the Brahmin converts who alone would be fully conversant with the complications of this language. After the Kushana kings a Hindu reaction set in, under King Kinnara many monasteries were destroyed, the rulers in general were Shivaites, and royal patronage was therefore withdrawn. During our period Kashmir gained a high reputation as a centre of Buddhist learning and nearly all the great Buddhist scholars between Aśvaghosa and Asanga are reported to have resided there at some time or other. Harivarman about 250 wrote his *Satyasiddhi*, an interesting synthesis of Maháyána and Hínayána views. Kashmiri monks went to Khotan, China and the Andhra country, and it was a Kashmiri monk, Gunavarman, who converted Java at the beginning of the fifth century.

4 CEYLON

At the beginning of our period a most significant discussion took place about the question whether learning or practice is the more important. The Dhammakathikas who stressed learning rather than practical realization were victorious and as a result the whole character of Ceylonese Buddhism changed. The learned monks were greatly honoured and in consequence all able and intelligent monks applied themselves to book-learning. The full-time practice of meditation was normally taken up by elderly monks of weak intellect and feeble physique. Book-learning soon included not only the Tipitaka, but also languages, grammar, history, logic, medicine, etc., the Buddhist monasteries became centres of learning and culture, and they were also made artistically attractive. In the first century BC Saddhátissa, the king's brother, had asked the monks to name even one holy man who deserved his veneration. The Sinhalese commentaries, on the other hand, assume that at that time the island was full of Arahats and for a long time afterwards many monks continued to live a strictly disciplined and austere spiritual life. As we know from Fa Hien and Yüan Tsang, Ceylon enjoyed a high reputation in other Buddhist lands.

During the fifth century three scholars, all non-Ceylonese from Southern India, translated the old Sinhalese commentaries into Páli. They were Buddhadatta, Buddhaghosa and Dhammapála. The most famous of them, Buddhaghosa, gave in his "Path to Purity" (*Visuddhimagga*) a splendid survey of Buddhist doctrine. The book is a compendium of the Tipitaka, one of the great masterpieces of Buddhist literature which describes authoritatively, lucidly and in great detail the principal meditational practices of the Buddhist Yogin. At the end of the fifth century also a council revised the text of the Tipitaka. From this time onwards the doctrine and tradition of the Theravádins has been definitely fixed. And about 400 the Páli Suttas had for the first time been translated into Sinhalese.

For its vitality the Buddhism of Ceylon continued to depend on its contact with India, but the nature of this contact had altered in the second period. The communications with the Western ports were now abandoned, and communications went through the ports at the mouth of the Ganges. In this way the influence of the monks of Magadha, particularly the Múlasarvástivádins, made itself felt.

There was during this period much discord and controversy between the two principal monasteries, the Mahávihára and the Abhayagirivihára, the latter having been founded in 24 BC. The Abhayagiri monks had a more democratic attitude to laymen, had more contact with India, were liberal in their views, welcomed new ideas from abroad, and were more progressive than the conservative Mahávihára monks. Soon after their foundation they received Vatsíputríya monks (see p. 30) from India. Later on they added to the basic Theraváda a superstructure of Maháyána doctrines and scriptures. At the end of the third century we hear of a new school among them, called Vaitulyaváda. This was probably a form of Maháyána, and in the fourth century Sanghamitra, an Indian Maháyánist "versed in the exorcism of spirits", won the support of the king, and the Mahávihára was closed for a time. But Sanghamitra was soon killed by a carpenter, and after 362 the Mahávihára began to function again. At this time, in AD 371, the left eye tooth of the Buddha was brought to Ceylon from Dantapura in Kalinga, and this precious relic was entrusted to the Abhayagiri monastery which because of its Maháyána leanings was more willing to encourage bhaktic piety. In the beginning of the fifth century Fa Hien counted 60,000 monks in Ceylon, of whom 5,000 belonged to the Abhayagiri, and 3,000 to the Mahávihára. The Ceylonese orthodoxy has succeeded in suppressing the entire literature of the Abhayagirivádins, but one of their works is preserved in a Chinese translation. It is Upatissa's *Vimuttimagga*, which has the same theme as Buddhaghosa's "Path to Purity", and was written before his time. It is curious to observe that it does not depart from Theravádin doctrines on any fundamental issues.

5 EXPANSION INTO GREATER ASIA

Five whole centuries had to elapse before Buddhism had pene-trated the Indian subcontinent, about as long as it took Rome to conquer the Italian peninsula. Now, about 500 years after the Buddha's Nirvana, His religion could begin to expand into Greater Asia. Gandhára, in the North-West of India, was the birthplace of Buddhism as a world religion. It was from here that the monks in the saffron robe gradually filtered into Central Asia, and from there into China, and further on. And it was chiefly the Maháyána form of Buddhism which took root outside India.

We must give some explanation why the Maháyánists were so much more effective missionaries than the Hínayánists. It was not that the latter were deficient in missionary zeal, but they were handicapped by the fact that they were rather inflex-ible literalists, whereas the Maháyána claimed much greater freedom in interpreting the letter of the Scriptures. This applied to both monastic rules and doctrinal propositions. For instance, if the rules about eating meat are strictly interpreted, nomadic populations will remain without the consolations of the Dharma, because among them the Vinaya rules cannot be strictly observed. Maháyána monks quickly found a way round unworkable rules, and reinterpreted them to fit the circum-stances. Of particular importance for the success of their missionary enterprises was their attitude to the Vinaya rule which forbids monks to practise medicine. The history of Christian missions in recent centuries shows that, violence apart, the medical missionaries effected more conversions than anyone else. The sword was the one method which the Buddhists disdained to use, but the scalpel, the herb and the potion opened to the Maháyánists the houses of the poor and rich alike. They convinced themselves that compassion and their responsibilities to their fellow-men counted for more than a well-meant monastic rule and they zealously gave themselves over to the study and practice of medicine, which formed part of the curriculum for instance at Nalanda University and also at the monastic institutions of Tibet.

The same latitudinarianism was practised with regard to doctrinal questions. Great care was taken to minimize the differences between Buddhist and non-Buddhist opinions, to absorb as much of the pre-existing views of their converts as was possible, be they Taoist, Bon, Shinto, Manichean or shamanistic. This latitudinarianism is of course in danger of lapsing into laxity in the moral and into arbitrary conjectures in the doctrinal field. The latter danger was on the whole more effectively avoided than the former and the best Maháyána literature contains little, if anything, that to any fair-minded Buddhist can appear as positively unorthodox. There was one factor which limited and restrained the "skill in means" of these men, and that was the fact that before they wrote their books their minds had been remoulded and disciplined by many years of meditation on traditional lines.

China was the first large country to be penetrated by Buddhist thought. As in Japan and Tibet later on, Buddhism went through five stages, which will act as our guides for the arrangement of our material.

1. There was first a period of consolidation, marked by translations of the basic texts.

2. This was followed by a preliminary attempt at coming to terms with the material. Buddhism did not move into a spiritual vacuum, but everywhere it encountered people formed by some previous tradition – by Taoism and Confucianism in China, Shinto in Japan, Bon in Tibet.

3. After this, the next, or third phase, is marked by a more mature assimilation of the doctrine, but still largely in dependence on Indian models. In China, for instance, this took the form of either numerous, generally brief, commentaries, or of original doctrinal treatises which were passed off as translations from the Sanskrit. Two of these are very well known. The one is the famous "Awakening of Faith", wrongly attributed to Aśvaghosa, and the other the so-called Śúrangama Sútra, said to have been brought from Nalanda, but actually written in China by Fang Jong.

4. We now come to the fourth phase, which is perhaps the most important of all and normally took 600 years to reach. A truly Chinese, Japanese and Tibetan Buddhism, which no longer did violence to the national character, asserted itself – in China with the Ch'an sect, in Japan in the Kamakura period, in Tibet with the Kahgyudpas and Gelugpas.

5. Then finally there is the period of decay. The first phase, as we saw, was one of bare copying; in the second one asserted one's independence, somewhat wilfully, as a child in its second year; in the third one attained some true independence, without however quite daring to, as in adolescence; in the fourth phase the native genius at last fully asserted itself. This child had grown up. The creative manhood of Buddhism lasted for several centuries. Manhood is followed by old age, and after a time the creative powers of Buddhism waned.

6 CENTRAL ASIA

Spreading from the Indo-Greek Bactrian kingdoms, Buddhism

had by the second century BC been well established in Central Asia. Khotan, Kucha, Turfan, etc., were at that time flourishing centres of culture, owing to the caravan routes which went through them. The establishment of Buddhism on the great silk routes was an event of decisive importance for its future propagation in Eastern Asia. Among the schools, the Sarvástiváda and Maháyána were most strongly represented. They brought their Scriptures with them and in the course of the twentieth

THE SPREAD OF BUDDHISM

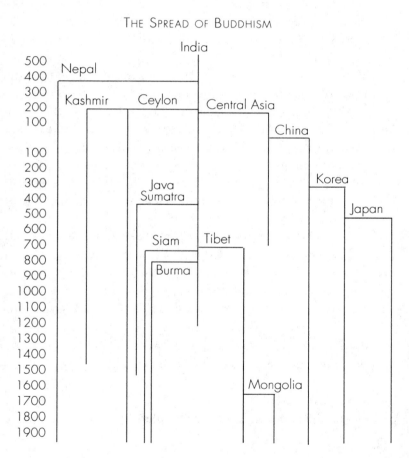

century European travellers have made many invaluable finds in the sands of Turkestan, which yielded both Indian books imported into Central Asia and translations of the Scriptures into the local languages, such as Sogdian, Khotanese, Kuchean, etc. We have also, in Kuchean, several works written in Kucha itself, imitating the Buddhist Sanskrit writings of India, but no really original works of local origin have come down to us. In addition these expeditions, carried out between 1900 and 1915, have brought to light a highly eclectic Buddhist art which offers a curious blend of Greco-Buddhist influences from Gandhara with others from the Roman Empire, and from Arsaco-Sassanid and Chinese Art. Through it the Greco-Buddhist art spread to China, where it led to the Wei art of the fifth century. In these cosmopolitan centres of intercontinental trade Buddhism was exposed to new religious influences which it had not encountered so far. It not only met with Christianity in its Nestorian form, but also with the Manicheans who were very active in that area, particularly among the Sogdians, and who left some traces on the Buddhist doctrines evolved there.

7 CHINA

From Central Asia Buddhism was brought, by a natural transi-tion, to China, which had conquered that region in the first century BC and kept it until the end of the Han dynasty (AD 220). The beginnings are said to go back to somewhere between 70 and 50 BC, and the religion slowly spread under the Han dynasty. But at first it was a foreign religion of the non-Chinese populations in China's outlying marches. In 148 a Parthian, Ngan Che Kao, and in 170 an Indian, Tshou Cho-fo, and a Yueh-chi, Tche tsh'an, arrived in China from Central Asia and established a monastery in Lo-yang, the capital of the Han. It was only in the period of disunity (221–589) which followed on the collapse of the Han, that Buddhism really became a major force in China itself. Only in 355 were Chinese for the first time permitted to become monks, at least in the realm of the Eastern Ts'in rulers. In the second century foreigners from Central Asia – Parthians, Sogdians, Indians, etc. – did some translations. In the third and fourth centuries Buddhism gained momentum among the people and at the Court, and some emperors clearly favoured it. By AD 400 1,300 works had been translated. Then came Kumárajíva, whose translations, made with the help of Chinese literati, were classical works and are still being read. By 500 Buddhism was firmly established throughout the whole of China and in a flourishing condition, with countless monasteries, temples, and sculptured grottoes for the monks.

This was a remarkable success for a religion which offended Chinese official sentiment at many points, for it seemed indifferent to the perpetuation of the family, showed little loyalty to the country and seemed to encourage baseless superstitions. The Buddhist clergy, on the ground that they had withdrawn from the world, refused to make the socially recognized signs of outward respect to the Son of Heaven and his representatives. All through its history, in fact, the Buddhist Church tended to develop into a state within the state. Their opponents blamed them for enjoying the benefits of the rule of the Son of Heaven without doing anything in return. The Buddhists claimed that on the contrary it is the monk, if anyone, who dispenses munificence, for enormous benefits accrue to the whole of society from his practice of the way of the Buddha. In fact, the benefits bestowed by the Son of Heaven are as but a drop of water when compared to the favours dispensed on all mankind by the Buddhist clergy. The state, however, always insisted on controlling the Buddhist

Church through the Ministry of Worship and saw to it that to some extent the monks lived up to their claim that they were sacrificing themselves for the good of the people.

The traditionalist opponents also stressed the foreign origin of Buddhism, which came from "barbarian lands", and the doctrine of reincarnation seemed to them quite incredible because they believed that when a man dies his soul also perishes. The problem of survival after death aroused intense interest at the time. In their polemics the Chinese Buddhists were apt to stray away from the orthodox denial of an individual soul and to postulate some enduring "spiritual something of the finest essence", which transmigrates from existence to existence. They quoted either Lao Tzu or the Yellow Emperor as having said that "the body suffers destruction, but the soul undergoes no change. With its unchangingness it rides upon changes and thus passes through endless transformations". This did not really well agree with Buddhism as it had been understood up to then.

The success was of course largely due to the fact that Buddhism contained a message which the indigenous teachers could not provide. For, as Seng-yu expressed it in the fifth century, "none of them have measured the shape of Heaven or peered into the mind of the Sage". Both the ruling classes and the people supported the new religion. The Emperors would be pleased to number as many peace-loving Buddhists as possible among their subjects, because Chinese society never knew universal conscription, and has always valued Peace very highly. The ruling layers of society would find the Buddhist priests more amenable than their Taoist rivals who were continually fomenting rebellions among the peasantry and whose churches were supported by contributions of the members who constituted them. The Buddhists, on the other hand, relied on the donations of wealthy laymen, and could therefore be relied upon not to pursue unwelcome political schemes of their own. The masses, finally, were greatly attracted to the Bodhisattva ideal which opened the highest possibilities even for those low on the social scale; the Buddhist pantheon, with merciful deities like Kuan Yin and others, brought encouragement and comfort; and from the support of the Buddha and Samgha they expected rewards in an after-life. It was widely believed in China that thereby one could influence Yama, the God of the Nether World. Some Buddhist priests, like for instance Buddha Mátanga in the third century, performed miracles, prophesied and cured diseases by means of their spells.

The development of Chinese Buddhist thought was largely determined by the choice of the sacred texts which were trans- lated into Chinese. Among the first and most influential were the Sútras on Prajñápáramitá. The mentality of the Chinese is said to be rationalistic, positivistic, matter-of-fact and anti- metaphysical. That this is only one side of their national character is shown by the enthusiastic reception which they gave to the highly metaphysical Prajñápáramitá literature from Han times onwards. The Bible was not studied with greater avidity in Protestant Europe than these very abstract writings on perfect wisdom and emptiness in China. Other works which gained a great popularity, and often became the nucleus of separate schools, were the *Lotus of the Good Law* (translations 250 onwards), which attracted the Chinese by the splendour of the scenery and by its parables, the story of *Vimalakírti* (transla- tions 188 onwards), which fascinated by the noble picture of a "white-robed" layman who took the sickness of the world upon himself, and the Nirvana Sútra (translation of 423) which seemed interesting for its teaching about the Buddha-nature within each of us. Between 200 and 450 there developed a strong interest in the technical details of Buddhist meditation, and many handbooks were translated during that period.

The rise of Buddhism coincided with the revival of Taoism, and many Chinese stressed the similarity in outlook between these intellectual trends. Few doubted that the Truth as it had been seen by the Buddha and the sages of China, by Lao-tzu and Chuang-tzu in particular, was one and the same. Until the fifth century, many Taoists considered Buddhism as one more method of reaching Taoist goals. In the third century Wang Fo wrote a famous pamphlet, in which he represented Buddhism as the result of "the conversion of the Barbarians by Lao-tzu".

Taoist terminology was often deliberately used to explain Buddhist concepts and in any case many of the Chinese equivalents of Sanskrit technical terms had first been used with a Taoist meaning, which to some extent influenced their use also in Buddhist contexts. A word like *tao*, used to translate *márga*, or "Path", would automatically carry with it many Taoist connotations and overtones quite unforeseen and unintended in the Sanskrit scriptures of India. *Shou-yi*, the equivalent of *satipatthána*, was often equated with the Taoist *Shou-yi*, meaning the retention of the flame of life; or *nairátmya*, translated as the "absence of *shen* (body)", was easily misunderstood as existence without a body, or in a spirit body; and "Emptiness" was identified with *pen-wu*, the "Original Non-existence" of Lao-tzu, the "Void filled to the brim", which, like a womb, carries all existence within it. To a representative thinker like Hui-Yüan the Dharmakáya is equivalent to the Highest Being, Personified Nature, the Sage or Great Man of the Neo-Taoists, the Buddha, the Spirit in the Centre of Existence, and the World Soul. Buddhist ideas were freely interpreted by the use of phrases taken from Lao-tzu, Chuang-tzu and the *Book of Changes* and it was quite usual to read the Taoist world-view into the Buddhist system. Less pronounced was the influence of Confucianism, which nevertheless made itself felt in the translation of the Sútras. During this period great care was taken to alter any sentiments or phrases which would offend the Confucian sense of propriety in such matters as family ethics, the relation between the sexes and the attitude to social superiors.

The main problem which interested the indigenous Buddhists during this period was taken from the Taoist tradition and concerned the relationship of being (*yu*) and non-being (*wu*), which later they identified with the "emptiness" (*Súnyatá*) of the Sanskrit writings. The discussion of this problem led to the emergence of *"the seven schools"*. Among these Tao-an's (312–85) School of Original Non-being taught that "non-being lies prior to the myriad kinds of evolution, and emptiness is at the beginning of the multitudinous shapes of physical things". The variations of this doctrine are counted as the second school. The third concentrated on the question of the emptiness of matter. The fourth teaches "the non-being of mind" which means "that the sage lacks any deliberate mind toward the ten thousand things; it does not mean that these things themselves are ever non-existent". This leads to the demand that we should "stop the activities of the mind within, and not let it be impeded by external matter", which is re-echoed in Chinese Buddhism again and again. The fifth, the "school of stored impressions", maintains that all phenomena are apparitions in a dream caused by mind and consciousness and will cease, together with the source, when we awaken from this dream. "Then the triple world is seen to be empty, and although the mind is extinguished, there is nothing it cannot produce." The sixth, called the "school of phenomenal illusion", taught that "all dharmas are equally illusory and, being so, constitute what pertains to ordinary truth. But the spirit (*shen*) of the mind is genuine and not empty, and as such pertains to the highest truth. For if this spirit were likewise empty, to whom could the Buddhist doctrine be taught and who would be there to cultivate its path, renounce the world and become a Sage? Hence we know that the Spirit is not empty." The seventh "school of causal combination" finally asserted that being, or worldly truth, results from the combination of causes and their disconnection leads to non-being, which is the highest truth.

About 400 *Kumárajíva's* scholarly work consolidated Buddhism and gave it greater prestige. He came from Kucha, born in 344 of an Indian father. Carried off as war booty to China in 384, he lived for fifteen years in Leang-chou in Kansu, and was taken in 402 to the capital of Chang-an, where he became Kuo-Shih, or Director of Religious Instruction, and died in 413. He enlisted the patronage of the emperor Yao Hsing, and translated more than a hundred works. Originally he was a Sarvástivádin monk, but later, while still in Kucha, he was converted to the doctrines of Nágárjuna.

His two most important disciples were Seng-chao (384–414) and Chu Tao-sheng (c. 360–434). Seng-chao's writings, collected under the title "Book of Chao", represent an interesting combination of Buddhism and Neo-Taoism. On this period the basic oppositions within Buddhist thinking were considered equivalent to those of Neo-Taoism. The contrast between the Absolute (*bhútatathatá*) and the temporal sequence of production and stopping seemed to correspond to that between non-being (*wu*) and being (*yu*); that between permanence and impermanence to that between quiescence (*ching*) and movement (*tung*); and the contrast between Nirvána and Samsára to that of non-activity (*wu wei*) and having activity (*yu wei*). Sengchao discussed the Buddhist philosophy of the Maháyána on the basis of these equivalences and his views are the first formulated indigenous Chinese Buddhist philosophical system which has come down to us.

Tao-sheng sounded one of the leitmotifs of Chinese Buddhism when he said: "Ever since the transmission of the scriptures eastward (i.e. to China), their translators have encountered repeated obstacles, and many have been blocked by holding too narrowly to the text, with the result that few have been able to see the complete meaning. Let them forget the fish-trap and catch the fish. Then one may begin to talk with them about the Way (*Tao*)." One of the questions which agitated the Chinese Buddhists of that time was that of the destiny of the Icchantikas. Are there any beings called *icchantikas* (a word of unknown etymological derivation), who are forever excluded from Buddhahood? Tao-sheng asserted, in opposition to most other scholars, that the *icchantikas* also possess the Buddha-nature and are therefore capable of achieving Buddhahood. During his own lifetime a fuller text of the *Great Nirvana Sútra* reached China and confirmed his views.

Tao-sheng also taught that "Buddhahood is achieved through instantaneous enlightenment". To his contemporaries this teaching appeared to be a "new doctrine", and the denial of a gradual enlightenment continued to be one of the special features of Chinese Buddhism. In the fifth century already Lu-cheng (425–94), a scholar-official, ascribed this difference in emphasis to a difference in national psychology. "The people of China have a facility for comprehending Truth intuitively or 'mirroring' it, but difficulty in acquiring learning. Therefore they close themselves to the idea of accumulating learning, but open themselves to that of one final ultimate. The Hindus, on the other hand, have a facility for acquiring learning, but difficulty in comprehending Truth intuitively. Therefore they close themselves to the idea of instantaneous comprehension, but open themselves to that of gradual enlightenment." In fact, Indian Buddhists had made a distinction between "gradual" and "sudden" enlightenment, but had regarded the second as the final stage of the first and nobody had thought of taking sides for one or the other. Tao-sheng now argues that, since the absolute emptiness of Nirvana is absolutely and totally different from all conditioned things, the enlightenment which mirrors it must also be totally different from all mental stages which are directed on other things. In consequence, enlightenment, if it is to be achieved at all, can be achieved only in its totality, and not in a gradual or piecemeal fashion. Many preparatory stages must, of course, precede the final flash of insight, but those ought to be called "learning"; they remain inside phenomenal existence and are not a part of the actual experience of enlightenment itself. For "when the single enlightenment comes, all the myriad impediments are equally brought to an end". The final vision is the total extinction of all ties, final liberation from them, for "what is genuine, that is permanent; what is temporary is false". From Tao-sheng's time onwards this theme was constantly debated in China and the theoreticians were divided into supporters of "gradual" or "instantaneous" enlightenment respectively.

So far about metaphysics. Popular faith, in its turn, was preoccupied with rebirth in Paradise. There were at that time three principal Paradises — that of the Buddha Akshobhya in the East, that of Amitábha in the West, and that of Maitreya at a future time on earth. The cult of *Akshobhya* is attested for Han times, and the faithful were advised to imitate him in never feeling wrath or anger for any being, in order that they may be reborn in Abhirati, His kingdom far away on a star in the East. In the course of time the cult of *Amitábha* proved more popular. It is said to have been first made known by the translations and preachings of the Arsacid prince An-Shih-Kao about AD 150. At the end of the fourth century, Hui-Yüan (334–416), a former Taoist, who even after his conversion to Buddhism still used Chuang-tzu's writings to explain his new faith, made the Lu-Feng monastery in Hupeh into a centre of the cult. In 402 a group of 124 persons was formed who prayed to be reborn in Amida's Paradise. This group was later on called the "Fellowship of the White Lotus" and was the prototype of the later Ching-t'u movement. Like the other Chinese schools, the Ching-t'u or "Pure Land" school was really founded only after AD 500. Akshobhya and Amitábha are cosmic Buddhas known only to the Maháyána. *Maitreya*, on the other hand, is the future Buddha due to appear on this earth, and he is known to both Maháyánists and Hínayánists. Sútras describing the splendour of the earth at the time of His coming were translated into Chinese in this our second period, but Maitreya's greatest popularity in China lay between c AD 400 and 650 and His cult seems to have been largely stimulated by the Yogácárin school.

CHAPTER

3

THE
THIRD PERIOD
AD 500–1000

1 INDIA

The most important event in India in this third period is the emergence of the *Tantra*. In addition we will have to say a few words about the *Pála synthesis* of Maháyána thought, the development of *logic*, and the doings of the *Hínayánists*.

The *Tantra* is the third, and last, creative achievement of Indian Buddhist thought. It went through roughly three phases. The first may be called *Mantrayána*. It began in the fourth century, gained momentum after AD 500, and what it did was to enrich Buddhism by the appurtenances of magical tradition, utilizing them for the purpose of facilitating the search for enlightenment. In this way many mantras, mudrás, mandalas and new deities were more or less unsystematically introduced into Buddhism. This was, after 750, followed by a systematization, called the *Vajrayána*, which co-ordinated all previous teachings with a group of Five Tathágatas. In the course of time, further trends and systems made their appearance. Noteworthy among them is the *Sahajayána*, which, like the Chinese Ch'an school, stressed meditational practices and the cultivation of intuition, taught by riddles, paradoxes and concrete images, and avoided the fate of turning into a dead scholasticism by holding on to no rigidly defined tenets. Towards the end of our period, in the tenth century, we have

the *Kálacakra*, "Wheel of Time", which is marked by the extent
of its syncretism and by its emphasis on astrology.

This new movement arose in the South and the North-
West of India. Non-Indian influences, from China, Central Asia
and the border lands round India, played a great part in
shaping it. There was also much absorption of ideas from abo-
riginal tribes within India itself. The Tantra endeavoured to
assign an honoured, though subordinate, role to all the spirits,
sprites, fairies, fiends, demons, ogres and ghosts which had
haunted the popular imagination, as well as to the magical
practices so dear to all nomadic and agricultural populations.
This further step in popularizing the religion aimed at
providing it with a more solid foundation in society. But as far
as the elite was concerned, there was the important difference
that non-Buddhists use magic to acquire power, whereas the
Buddhists do so to free themselves from the powers alien to
their own true being.

The Tantra departed from the early Maháyána in its definition of the goal and of the ideal type of person and also in its
method of teaching. The aim is still Buddhahood, though no
longer at a distant future, aeons and aeons hence, but
Buddhahood right now, "in this very body", "in the course of
one single thought", achieved miraculously by means of a new,
quick and easy way. The ideal saint is now the *Siddha*, or
magician, who has, however, some resemblance to a
Bodhisattva as he was said to be after the eighth stage (see p.
47), with his wonder-working powers fully developed.

As for the method of teaching, the Maháyána had stated its
doctrines in *Sútras* and *Sástras* which were public documents,
available to anyone sufficiently interested to procure, and sufficiently intelligent to understand them. In their stead we now
witness the composition of a new vast canonical literature of

Tantras, which are secret documents destined only for a chosen few who are properly initiated by a *guru*, or teacher, and which are phrased in a deliberately mysterious and ambiguous language, meaningless in itself without the oral explanations of a teacher who had been properly initiated into its secrets. The secret has been well kept, and although thousands of Tantras are still extant, modern scholars seldom have a clue to their meaning, partly because, hypnotized by the "scientific" assumptions of their own age, they have little sympathy with magical modes of thinking. The general principles of Tantric teaching can be inferred with some certainty, but the concrete detail, which is bound up with actual yogic practices and constituted the real message, eludes our grasp. Unlike the early Maháyánists (see p. 42), the Tantric authors no longer link their scriptures with Śákymuni, but frankly assign them to some mythical Buddha who is said to have preached them at some remote and distant past.

The foundations for these new literary conventions were laid already in the Yogácára school. That school systematizes the experiences gained in the course of an excessively introverted transic meditation, and the Yogins were convinced that the visions they had in trance had much greater reality than what we call "facts", than dates or localities, than individuals, their names and biographies. In consequence they tell us that certain works are due to the inspiration of, say, "Maitreya" and forget to mention the individual name of the human author who took down the inspiration. They thus cause great difficulties to modern historical research, though in their own view they tell us all that is essential and needful. The Yogácárins had also for a long time shown a keen interest in the more secretive modes of conveying information, and Asanga's *Maháyánasamgraha* contains a fine classification of the permissible ways

77

by which a "hidden meaning" may be conveyed, when one says something different from what one really wants to say. It was in fact from the Yogácára branch of the Maháyána that the Tantric ideas and practices originated.

The new trend was bound to weaken the monastic system. By fostering the development of small conventicles of disciples who owed absolute submission to their *guru* it favoured the dispersal of the Samgha into self-sufficient bands of Yogins, many of whom believed that they were spiritually so developed as not to need the restraint of the monastic rules any longer, while others by their unconventional behaviour liked to cock a snook at the sheltered lives of the ordinary monks.

The mantrayanic development was originally a natural reaction against the increasingly adverse historical trends which threatened to suffocate Indian Buddhism. In their defence and for their protection its adherents now more and more mobilized magical and occult powers and invoked the help of more and more mythological beings, whose actual reality was attested to them in the practice of transic meditation. Among these great attention was paid to the "wrathful" deities, like the "Protectors of the Dharma", also called *vidyárájá*, "kings of the sacred lore", who are inherently well-meaning, but assume a terrifying appearance to protect the faithful. It is also interesting to note that in their search for security the Buddhists of that time more and more relied on feminine deities. Already about AD 400 Tárá and Prajñápáramitá had been adored as celestial Bodhisattvas. They were soon joined by the "Five Protectresses", with Mahámáyurí, "the great Pea Hen", at their head. Later on the practitioners of advanced mystical meditation evolved a whole pantheon of feminine deities, like Cundá, Vasudhará, Usnísavijayá, Vajravárahí, Buddhalocaña, and others; the practitioners of the magical arts were especially devoted to the "Queens of the sacred Lore" and to the dákinís, or "sky walkers"; and the general population was encouraged to turn for their own specific interests to goddesses who gave children, protected from the small-pox and so on. After 700 the so-called "left-handed" Tantra added consorts of the Buddhas and Bodhisattvas. These were called *Vidyás* of *Prajñás*, corresponding literally to the *Ennoias* and *Sophias* of the Gnostics. A seemingly erotic ritual often accompanied the cult of the vidyás, and this aspect of the Tantra has greatly bemused the more unsophisticated European enquirers. Nothing need be said about it here, because the actual facts of this ritual are totally unknown to us.

The belief in the occult, in magic and miracles, has at all times been an integral part of Buddhism, though more by way of recognizing an established fact than as a matter of urgent practical importance. But as the spiritual potency of the Dharma waned and as history was felt to become more and more adverse, greater reliance was placed on magic to ward off dangers and secure help. We find that after AD 300 sporadically *mantras* of all kinds are slowly incorporated into the holy writings. These were also called *dháranís*, from the root *dhr*, because they are intended to "uphold" or "sustain" the religious life. Then, after AD 500, all the customary procedures of magic were resorted to, rituals as well as magical circles and diagrams. These were employed to both guard the spiritual life of the elite, and to give to the unspiritual multitude that which it desired. Mudrás, or ritual gestures, often reinforced the efficacy of the spells.

Moreover there are the *mandalas*, the harmonious beauty of which still appeals to our aesthetic sense. Magical circles, which mark off a sacred or ritually pure spot, are, of course, as old as magic and go back well into prehistoric times. The peculiar Buddhist arrangement of mandalas seems, however, to have developed in Central Asia and owes much to the pattern of the Chinese TLV mirrors of the Han dynasty. The mandala expresses cosmic and spiritual forces in a mythological, or per-sonified, form, representing them by the images of deities, shown either in their visual appearance, or by the syllable which allows us to evoke them and which constitutes their occult principle. These symbols, properly read, allow us to give expression to deeply hidden fears, primordial impulses and archaic passions. Through them we can chain, dominate and dissolve the forces of the universe, effect a revulsion from all the illusory things of the samsaric world, and achieve reunion with the light of the one absolute Mind. Mandalas are a special form of age-old diagrams of the cosmos, considered as a vital process which develops from one essential principle and which rotates round one central axis, Mount Sumeru, the *axis mundi*. Such diagrams were reproduced not only in mandalas, but also in ritual vases, royal palaces, Stupas and Temples. Owing to the equivalence of macrocosm and microcosm, the drama of the universe is reproduced in each individual, whose mind, as well as whose body, can be regarded as a *mandala*, as the scene of the quest for enlightenment. The construction and designing of *mandalas*, and the evocation of deities, were naturally governed by strict rules and well defined ritual observances.

The creative outburst of the early Tantra led to a complete chaos of assumptions about cosmic and spiritual forces and it was the *Vajrayána* which imposed order on the vast inchoate mass of traditions which had evolved. It adopted a fivefold division of all cosmic forces, each class being in a sense presided over by one out of five Tathágatas. The names of the Five Tathágatas were Vairocana, Akshobhya, Ratnasambhava,

Amitábha and Amoghasiddhi. A complicated and most intricate system of magical correspondences, identifications, transformations and transfigurations then link all the forces and facts of the universe with these five "families". The body in particular is regarded as a microcosm, which embodies the entire universe and is the medium for realizing the truth, very largely by methods which form a part of what is nowadays known as *Hathayoga* in India. We hear much about parallelisms between the visible, the audible and the touchable, and everything is designed to unite the powers of mind, speech and body for the purpose of realizing the final state of completeness, or enlightenment. The Vajrayána has been well defined as "the art of living which enables us to utilize each activity of body, speech and mind as an aid on the Path to Liberation", and in this way it is astonishingly akin to the contemporary Ch'an school. The true meaning of Vajrayána teachings is, however, not always easy to ascertain, because here it has become a convention to clothe the highest into the form of the lowest, to make the most sacred appear as the most ordinary, the most transcendent as the most earthly, and the sanest knowledge is disguised by the most grotesque paradoxes. This is a deliberate shock therapy directed against the over-intellectualization of Buddhism at that time. The abundant sexual imagery in particular was intended to shock monkish prudery. Enlightenment, the result of a combination of wisdom and skill in means, is represented by the union of female and male in the ecstasy of love. Their becoming one in enlightenment is the highest indescribable happiness (*mahásukha*).

The further development of Buddhism in Northern India was greatly influenced by the accidents of royal patronage. In the seventh century, King Harshavardhana, a lesser Aśoka, patronized Buddhism, preferring first the Sammitíyas, and then, perhaps as a result of Yüan-tsang's visit in 630–44, the Maháyána, though Shivaism may have been his own personal religion. It was, however, the *Pála* dynasty of Bengal (750–1150) who by their support of the great Buddhist universities determined the history of Buddhism for centuries to come. From the sixth to the ninth centuries, Nalanda had been the centre of living thought for the entire Buddhist world. Under the Pála dynasty new centres were founded in Eastern India, especially Vikramasíla, and Odantapuri. These together with Jaggadala and Somarúpa were the focal points from which Buddhist culture radiated over Asia during the ninth to twelfth centuries.

I-Tsing, who visited Nalanda about AD 700, said of the sects there that "they rest in their own places, and do not get themselves embroiled with one another". In fact, the official Buddhism of the period became a mixture of *Prajñápáramitá* and *Tantra*. King Dharmapála (*c.* 770–810), immediately on ascending the throne, greatly honoured the teacher Haribhadra, a leading authority on *Prajñápáramitá* and *Abhisamayálankára*, while not at the same time neglecting the interpreters of the *Guhyasamája*, a celebrated Tantric text. The monks of these universities combined metaphysics and magic almost like the *Gerbert of Rheims* and *Albert the Great* of mediaeval folklore. Their range of interest is well typified by what Táranátha reports of one of them. "By constantly looking on the face of the holy Tárá he resolved all his doubts. He erected eight religious schools for the *Prajñápáramitá*, four for the exposition of *Guhyasamája*, one each for each one of three kinds of Tantra, and he also established many religious schools with provisions for teaching the *Mádhyamika* logic. He conjured up large quantities of the elixir of life, and distributed it to others, so that old people, 150 years old and more, became young again." This *Pála synthesis* of Maháyána thought has shown an astounding vitality. Though destroyed by the Muslims in Bengal, it spread to Java and Nepal, and in Tibet it continued as a living tradition up to recent years.

As the Buddhists preceded the Hindus in the development of Tantras, so also in that of *logic*. The social standing, as well as the income, of religious groups in the Indian Middle Ages depended to some extent on the showing they could make in the religious disputations which were about as popular at that time as tournaments were in the European Middle Ages. In this context, a knowledge of the rules by which valid can be distinguished from invalid inferences would be a definite advantage. Just as the disputes of the Greek sophists led to the logical systems of the Socratic schools, so disputes of the Indian religious sects led to the formulation of logical and epistemological theories among the Buddhists. This new trend goes back to Nágárjuna, but the first Buddhist to teach an articulate system of logic was Dinnága (*c.* 450), a pupil of Asanga. He also initiated systematic epistemological studies among the Buddhists, discussing the sources of knowledge, the validity of perception and inference, as well as the object of knowledge, and the reality of the external world. In the course of this third period these logical studies reached great maturity with Dharmakírti (*c.* 600–50) and Dharmottara (*c.* 850), who dealt with many of the problems which have occupied modern European philosophy, such as the problem of solipsism and the existence of other minds. This interest continues right to the end of Buddhism in India, and it was from there carried to Tibet and to a lesser extent to China and Japan. The logical studies of the Yogácárins developed quite naturally from some of the questions which the Vaibháshikas (see p. 56) had asked themselves and they kept Buddhist philosophical thinking abreast, and often ahead, of the time.

In India itself the Maháyánists appear to have remained numerically a minority. In AD 640, for instance, out of 250,000 monks counted by Yúan-tsang, only 70,000 to 100,000 belonged to the Maháyána. It must seem definitely unfair therefore that I can find nothing to say about the Hínayánists, and that all the space is given to their Maháyána rivals. This disproportion is perhaps due to a fault in perspective which affects most historical works. The continuing tradition, however praiseworthy, is taken for granted and passed over without comment. The life sprouting out at the growing points gets all the limelight. By way of correction it is sometimes good to remember that at any given time the majority of Buddhists were virtuous people who just carried on in the old ways, and who have no news value, just as virtuous women are said to have none.

2 NEPAL AND KASHMIR

The Buddhism of *Nepal* continued to flourish as an offshoot of that of Northern India, and Patan became a replica of one of the Pála universities. Between the seventh and ninth centuries close ties were developing with Tibet, and many Tibetans came to Nepal to learn about the Buddhism of India. It was in Nepal that Śántaraksita encountered Padmasambhava when he conveyed to him the invitation of the king of Tibet.

At the beginning of this period, the Samgha of *Kashmir* suffered a serious setback from the invasions of the Huns, who under Mihirkula (c. 515) devastated the country and persecuted the monks. After their departure Meghavahana, a Buddhist ruler, forbade all slaughter of animals, while compensating butchers and fishermen for the resulting loss. This king erected many religious buildings and his successors continued to patronize the Church. Yüan-tsang remained for two years in

Kashmir. He found about 5,000 monks, but noted that "at the present time this kingdom is not much given to the faith". New prosperity began in the seventh and eighth centuries with the Karkota rulers. The faith revived again, though in a form which brought it nearer to Hindu cults. This shows itself in Sarvajñamitra, and his Hymns in praise of Tárá. Sorcery and miracle-working spread and the monks practised how to make or stop rain, how to check the flow of flooded rivers, etc. The spread of Tantrism and Devotionalism brought Buddhism nearer to Śivaism, which in its turn in the ninth and tenth centuries developed, with Vasugupta and others, firm philosophical foundations. About 1,000 we have Kshemendra, who wrote Avadánas, Buddhist legends resembling Brahminic Mahátmyas. In the ninth century many Kashmiri monks went to Tibet.

3 CEYLON

At this time the Theravádin sect managed to expand beyond Ceylon itself on the route between Ceylon and the places of pilgrimage in Magadha, and many were found in Southern India and in the region of the two ports through which they went, i.e. the Ganges delta (Támralipti) in the East and Bharukaccha in the West. In Ceylon itself the Abhidhamma was greatly honoured, but at the same time magical practices began to be encouraged. About 660 we hear for the first time of the chanting of *Paritta* as a ceremony, which became a regular feature of later Buddhism in Ceylon.

For a time the Maháyána was fairly strong, and both Prajñápáramitá and Tantra had their centres in the island. The Indikutasaya Copper Plates have preserved for us parts of one of the large Prajñápáramitá Sútras in Sinhalese script of the eighth or ninth century. The Abhayagiri continued to import many Maháyána features and its relations to the Mahávihára remained unfriendly. About 620 the members of the Mahávihára refused the king's request that they should hold the *uposatha*-ceremony together with those of the Abhayagiri, and about 650 the Mahávihára were so incensed with the king for the favours he bestowed on the Abhayagiri that they applied to him the "turning down of the alms-bowl", an act equivalent to the excommunication of a layman. In 536 a book called *Dharmadhátu* was brought to Ceylon, which probably dealt with the Three Bodies of the Buddha and this book was greatly honoured by the king and became an object of ritual worship. In the ninth century Vajrayána tenets were spread by an Indian monk residing in Abhayagiri and the king was greatly attracted to the teaching. In the words of the Chronicle, "it also became prevalent among the foolish and ignorant people of this country" and led to the formation of a special order of monks clad in dark blue robes. During the seventh century an ascetic reaction against the generally comfortable life of the monks made itself felt at the Abhayagiri. Those who strove to revive the rigours of old separated themselves in the ninth century and as *Pamsukúlikas* they were prominent for centuries, deriving their name from the ancient practice of wearing robes made from rags collected on rubbish heaps. In the Polonnaruva period, from the end of the eighth century onwards, Hindu influences on Buddhist practices began to come in.

4 CENTRAL ASIA

Under the T'ang dynasty, Central Asia once more became an intermediary between China and India, for between 692 and c. 800 it was again part of the Chinese empire. The Tibetans held sway for some time and many valuable Tibetan documents from Tun-huang, etc., dating from the seventh to tenth centuries, have been recovered in recent years. The empire of the Uigurs, at its height between 744 and 840, is also of some importance for the history of Buddhism. Defeated in 840 by the Kirghiz, the Uigurs then founded a new kingdom in the region of Turfan, Bechbaliq, Karachar and Kucha, which persisted in Turfan and some other areas until the fourteenth century. The Uigurs, from the eighth century onwards Manicheans, were in the ninth century converted to Buddhism and an abundance of Buddhist works was translated into Uigur from the Sanskrit, Kuchean, Khotanese and Chinese. Generally speaking, however, after 900 Turkish Islamic populations displaced the Buddhist Indo-Europeans in Central Asia.

5 SOUTH-EAST ASIA

Buddhism reached South-East Asia as the result of the colonizing activities of Hindus, who not only founded trading stations, but also brought their cults and culture with them. From the third century onwards the area, also known as "Further India", was increasingly ruled by dynasties which could either claim Indian descent, or which were at least motivated by the ideals of Hindu civilization.

By the fifth and sixth century both Maháyána and Hínayána Buddhism had filtered into *Burma*. At first it came from the Pallava country of Southern India (Magadha) and the Sarvástivádins may well have established themselves for a time. From the ninth century onwards, Pála Buddhism was imported from Bihar and Bengal. It led in Burma to the formation of a powerful organization of monks who called themselves "Aris" (from *árya*, "noble"). We have no information about their metaphysical teachings, but we know that they worshipped the Maháyána pantheon, were addicted to Tantric practices, justified doctrinal innovations by occasionally discovering some "hidden scripture" and absorbed many local customs, for instance the *jus primae noctis*, which they considered as an act of religious worship.

Turning to *Indo-China*, we find that in Cambodia about AD 400 already the reigning house, the nobility and the priesthood are Hindus. We also find a mixture of Śivaism and Mahāyāna first in Fu-nan, and then, after 540, in the Khmer kingdom, of which Angkor became the capital in 802. The Khmers erected many huge buildings, some of which were devoted to Mahāyāna deities, among whom Lokeśvara and Bhaisajyaguru were specially popular. Up to about AD 1000 the syncretism of Śivaism and Mahāyāna also dominated the Champa kingdom, although the Mahāyāna element was less strong there, and also the Sammitīyas and Sarvāstivādins were represented. The influence of Śrīvijaya greatly strengthened the Mahāyāna during the ninth century also in Indo-China.

Indonesia was likewise ruled by Indian emigrants, and a Buddhism imported from South-East India is attested there from the fifth century onwards. The imperial power of Śrīvijaya after 675 replaces by Buddhism the Brahminism prevalent until then. In Sumatra the Sarvāstivādins were strong in the seventh century. Later on the Vajrayāna was brought in from the Pāla Universities. The same happened in Central Java under the Śailendra dynasty from the eighth century onwards, although Śivaism always remained fairly strong. The Śailendras filled the Kedu plain with beautiful temples, adorned with exceptionally fine sculptures. The most famous of these is the gigantic Borobudur, a Stūpa built in the sixth century, which is a *mandala* in stone, and symbolizes the cosmos as well as the way to salvation. Those who walk in *pradaksinā* through its galleries will thereby ritually undergo the process of moving out of Samsara into Nirvana, ascending through the three levels of the triple world to the supramundane transcendental realm. Some of the great Maháyána texts are here illustrated on bas-reliefs, i.e. the *Játakamálá, Lalitavistara, Gandavyúha* and *Karmavibhanga*.

6 CHINA AND KOREA

The three centuries between 500 and 800 were the most prosperous and creative years for Chinese Buddhism. The religion was now assimilated, and became an integral part of national life. Eight indigenous schools arose during this period. They were (1) the Lü-tsung, founded by Tao-Hsüan (595–667); (2) the San-lun, founded by Chi-tsang (549–623); (3) the Weih-shih, founded by Yüan-tsang (596–664); (4) the Mi-tsung, founded by Amoghavajra (705–74); (5) the Hua-yen tsung, founded by Tu-shun (557–640); (6) the T'ien-t'ai, founded by Chih-k'ai (538–597); (7) the Ching-t'u, founded by Shan-tao (613–81); and (8) the Ch'an school, said to have been founded by Bodhidharma about 520.

The first school, or *Vinaya* sect, had no doctrinal significance, its purpose being to work for a stricter observance of the Vinaya rules, particularly as regards ordination and the begging of food. The school had some success in raising the standards of monastic strictness, but it soon passed to the periphery of the Buddhist world.

The next three schools are Indian scholastic systems, which remained more or less foreign bodies in Chinese Buddhism and did not endure for more than a few centuries. The *San-lun* is the Chinese form of the Mádhyamikas. It is based, as the name says, on "three treatises", one by Nágárjuna and two by Áryadeva, and continues the work done by Kumárajíva about 400. Chi-tsang, its founder, was a most prolific writer of books, chiefly commentaries and encyclopaedias. The general purpose of the school is to discard all views, so that emptiness may prevail.

The *Weih-Shih* is the Chinese form of the Yogácárins and its basic textbook is the *Ch'eng Weih-shih Lun*, "The Completion of the Doctrine of mere ideation". The great pilgrim Yüan-tsang had brought with him from Nálandá ten commentaries to Vasubandhu's "Thirty Stanzas", and he combined them into one work, generally giving preference to the interpretations of Dharmapála (sixth century). It is the purpose of this school to discard all objects, to see that they all "are mental representations dependent upon the evolutions of consciousness", and to merge into the one Mind in which everything is mere ideation. Its tenets and attitudes were, however, not in harmony with the general tendencies of Chinese mentality. In K'uei-chi (632–82), Yüan-tsang's leading disciple, this school attracted another first-class mind, but soon it degenerated into scholastic disputes about the "seventh", "eighth" and "ninth" consciousness, which generally did nothing but reflect divergent Indian traditions, not always clearly understood.

The *Mi-tsung*, or "School of the Mysteries", is the Chinese form of the Tantra. It is also known as Chen-yen, the school of the "Mantras". In the eighth century, three Indians, Śubhákarasimha (637–735), Vajrabodhi (670–741) and Amoghavajra (705–74), imported into China Tantric systems of the non-Shaktic type, and won great influence at the Court of the T'ang emperors. They there established a great variety of rites, partly designed to avert catastrophes from the Empire, and partly to favourably influence the fate of people after their death. The school lasted not much longer than a century, and in later times the Tantric tradition in China fell into the hands of Lama monks from Tibet.

The next three schools attained a greater degree of assimilation. First among these is the *Hua-yen-tsung*, literally the "Wreath" school, which represents the link between Yogácára and Tantra, in that it gives a cosmic interpretation to the ontological ideas of the Yogácárins. It is derived from a study of the Indian *Avatamsaka Sútra*. Here the sameness, or identity, of everything is interpreted as the interpenetration of every element in the world with every other element. The one principle of the cosmos is present in all beings and in all things, in the sense that everything harmonizes with everything else. Each particle of dust contains all the Buddha-lands, and each thought refers to all that was, is and will be. The sensory universe is a reflex of the eternal and the mysteries of the truth can be beheld everywhere. Unlike the Tantra this school did not aim at the manipulation and control of cosmic forces by magical means, but was content with the contemplation and aesthetic appreciation of the interplay of these forces. This doctrine greatly influenced the attitude to nature in the Far East, and also inspired many artists in China and later on in Japan. The Hua Yen school, founded about 630, lasted until about AD 1000.

One of its greatest teachers was *Fa-tsang* (643–712), the descendant of a Sogdian family and originally a disciple of Yüan-tsang, who wrote an important work called "Meditation which extinguishes false imaginations, and by which one returns to the source". With the Yogácárins he speaks of one mind which makes possible the world of particulars. But then he goes beyond the Yogácárin doctrine by claiming that everything has the following three marks, or characteristics:

1. Existentially, each particular object, each "particle of dust", contains in itself the whole realm of reality (dharmadhátu) in its entirety;
2. Creationally it can generate all possible kinds of virtue, and any object may therefore reveal the secrets of the entire world;

3. In each particle the emptiness of true reality is perceivable.

Six kinds of contemplation are recommended to the disciple:

1. To look into the serenity of Mind to which all things return;
2. To realize that the world of particulars exists because of the One Mind;
3. To observe the perfect and mysterious interpenetration of all things;
4. To observe that there is nothing but Suchness;
5. To observe that the mirror of Sameness reflects the images of all things, which thereby do not obstruct each other;
6. To observe that, when one particular object is picked up, all the others are picked up with it.

The *T'ien-t'ai* school is so called because its founder, Chih-k'ai, lived and taught in the T'ien-t'ai mountains in Chekiang. It is also known as the *Fa-hua*, or "Lotus" school, because it took the *Saddharmapundaríka* as its basic text. Chih-k'ai wrote some extremely valuable treatises on the art of meditation. In its doctrines the T'ien-t'ai aimed at a syncretism of all the different Maháyána schools and in its general policy it tended to promote social order in collaboration with the secular authorities. Its mentality is akin to that of the Yellow Church of Tibet, although Chinese conditions produced constant checks on its political influence. In its profound and complicated philosophical teachings the T'ien-t'ai shows strong traces of the influence not only of the Weih-shih and Hua-yen schools, but also of the *Awakening of Faith in the Maháyána*, a work falsely ascribed to Aśvaghosha, which may very well have originated in China. The T'ien-t'ai had a strong preference for calling the Absolute "true or genuine Suchness" or also the "Womb of the Tathágata", which contains within itself all the pure and impure potentialities and is thus capable of generating both this-worldly and other-worldly things.

This dualistic theory is special to the T'ien't'ai school. All things and events of the phenomenal world are "harmoniously integrated", and there is no barrier between one thing and another. The T'ien-t'ai tend to ascribe a greater degree of reality to the phenomenal world than the Indian schools would allow. In their concern with social activity they emphasized that Nirvana eliminates all ills but not likewise "the great functioning" of the universe. According to them even the Buddhas can work and stay within the circle of birth and death, because even after enlightenment they retain their impure potentialities, which cannot ever be destroyed and therefore they may, like ordinary people, be engaged in impure or mundane acts. And because every single thing contains the absolute Mind in its totality, not only, as Tao-sheng had said (see p. 72), all sentient beings have the Buddha-nature in them, but also, as Chan-jan (711–82), the ninth patriarch of the T'ien-t'ai explained, "even inanimate things possess the Buddha-nature", "and why should exception be made of even a tiny particle of dust?"

In the Ching-t'u ("Pure Land") school *Amidism*, which had for centuries existed as a popular trend (see p. 74), became more strictly organized. This school was founded by Tao-ch'o (562–645), and consolidated by Shan-tao (613–81). These two were followed by a few more outstanding figures, called "patriarchs", the last of whom, Shao-k'ang, died in 805. After the ninth century Amidism ceases to have a separate corporate existence as a sect and becomes an influence which pervades all forms of Buddhism in China.

Amidism taught that the power inherent in the name of the
Buddha Amitábha can remove all obstacles to salvation and that
the mere utterance of His name (O-mi-to-fo) can assure rebirth
in His kingdom. The legend of Amitábha is based chiefly on
the *Sukhávatívyúha*, a Sanskrit text of the first century AD. It tells
us that inconceivable aeons ago the Bodhisattva Dharmákara
made forty-eight vows, among them the promise that all who
call on his name shall be saved; that later on he became the
Buddha Amitábha; and that finally, ten aeons ago, in accordance with his vows, he established the Pure Land or Western
Paradise which lies one million billion Buddha-lands away. This
sect honoured Amitábha by multiplying copies of His statues as
well as of the Sútras which deal with Him, and also by
paintings which depict and by hymns which sing the splendours of the Pure Land. A study of the dated inscriptions at
Long-men shows that the cult of Amitábha flourished there
particularly between 647 and 715. The Amidists also worshipped Kuan-yin, the Indian Avalokiteśvara, who in the course
of time changed his sex in China, and became a feminine deity.

The strength of Amidism lies in its democratic spirit. The
intellectualism of religious aristocrats who retire into solitary
mountain places is quite beyond the reach of the common
people who must live in the bustle of ordinary life. A religion
which appeals to the masses must above all aim at extreme simplification, and the great merit of the Ching-t'u teaching,
according to its propounders, is that it is simple and easy to
follow. All that is required by way of virtue is just faith, and the
Ching-t'u authors seem to assume that that is more commonly
found than the capacity for trance or wisdom.

The most important of all Chinese schools is, however, the
Ch'an school. It is the fourth and last of the original recreations
of the Buddha's thought, the first three being the Abhidharma,

the Maháyána and the Tantra. With the Tantra Ch'an is nearly contemporary and the two have much in common. The history of the Ch'an school begins with Hui-neng (638–713), also known as the "sixth Patriarch". Before Hui-neng we have a kind of pre-history of Ch'an, which is said to begin with Bodhidharma, a more or less legendary Southern Indian who came to China at the beginning of the sixth century and spent nine years in Lo-yang, the capital, in "wall-gazing". The importance of Bodhidharma lies in providing the Ch'an sect with a concrete link with the Indian tradition, a link which the school in spite of its profound originality greatly cherished. The Buddha Śákyamuni, so we are told, had given the secret doctrine to Mahákáśyapa, and from him it was transmitted to one "patriarch" after the other, but "from mind to mind, without the use of written texts", until it reached Bodhidharma, the twenty-eighth of the line. Between Bodhidharma and Hui-neng we have four more "patriarchs" who taught a Buddhism strongly tinged with Taoism in the tradition of Tao-sheng (see pp. 71–3). Among them the third patriarch, Seng-t'san (died 606), is noteworthy for his superb poem on "Believing in Mind", which is one of the great classics of Buddhist literature. These patriarchs had, however, little influence on society in general, because they lived in poverty without a fixed residence and generally made it a rule not to spend more than one night in any one place.

History further records that the interpretation of the teachings of these patriarchs led to a rift between a Northern branch, headed by Shen-hsiu (c. 600–706), and a Southern branch, headed by Hui-neng, of Canton, the main point in dispute being the question of "gradual" and "sudden" enlightenment. The Northern followers of "gradual enlightenment", who assumed that our defilements must be gradually removed by strenuous practice, soon died out. What we call the Ch'an school consists of Hui-neng's numerous disciples. Organizationally, Ch'an became independent only at the time of Pochang Huai-hai (720–814). Up to then, most Ch'an monks had lived in monasteries of the Lü-tsung under the regulations of its Vinaya. Now Po-chang made a new set of rules for Ch'an monks, which tried to revive the austerity and simplicity of living conditions in the early Order, and also combined the Buddhist Vinaya with Confucian rules of etiquette. The regulations of all Ch'an monasteries are derived from Po-chang. He introduced an innovation which did much to ensure the survival and social success of his sect. The monks went on their begging round each morning, but in addition they were expected to work. "A day without work, a day without eating" was Po-chang's watchword. This was something unheard of so far. The Ch'an school has had two periods of vigorous development, the first in the T'ang, the second in the Sung period. The second phase belongs to chapter IV, and here we confine ourselves to the first.

It had long been a problem whether learning or practical realization is more important. The Ch'an sect, as against the Ceylonese Dhammakathikas (see p. 59), uncompromisingly decided in favour of practical realization. They found a situation in which the fervour of the faithful had so multiplied the means of salvation, in the form of Sútras, commentaries, philosophical subtleties, images and rites, that the goal itself was apt to be lost sight of; the spiritual life was in danger of being choked by the very things which were designed to foster it. In their reaction against the overgrown apparatus of piety they advocated a radical simplification of the approach to enlightenment. They never tired of denouncing the misuse of this apparatus, which could so easily have become an end in itself. In particular they set themselves against the excessive worship paid to the scriptural traditions and insisted that salvation could not be found by the study of books. That did not mean that they studied no books at all. On the contrary their own sayings are saturated with references to such works as the *Vajracchediká Sútra*, and the *Lankávatára Sútra*, the two favourites of the school in its early days. But they felt strongly that the study of these Sútras should play only quite a subordinate role compared with the demands of meditation (*Ch'an* means *dhyána*) and spiritual realization. The complicated cosmological and psychological theories of the other Buddhist schools are rejected as just so much "rubbish" and "useless furniture".

By way of protest against the excesses of devotion and the current misunderstandings of the Buddha's role, a famous Ch'an master of the T'ang dynasty, Tan-hsia T'ien-jan, in the eighth century, when he was cold, burned a statue of the Buddha and warmed himself by it. Because a definite fixation of the affections on a definite object might act as a fetter, another Ch'an master coldly informs us that, if you meet the Buddha, you ought to kill Him if He gets in your way. Less drastic are the replies of another Ch'an master Nan-yuan Hui-yung, to the question, "What is the Buddha?" He just said, "What is not the Buddha?", or "I never knew Him", or "Wait until there is one, then I will tell you". All this hardly gives the mind very much to rest upon. Ch'an was intent on restoring Buddhism as a spiritual doctrine. Spiritual things have their own laws, their own dimensions, and their own mode of being. This makes them rather indefinite for mundane perception, and it has been rightly said that the spirit can be apprehended only by the eyes of the Spirit.

The Ch'an school well knew that it represented a quite new departure. Just as the Tantric followers of Padmasambhava regarded him as a second Buddha, equal in authority to Śákyamuni, so in the same spirit the Ch'an Buddhists deliberately called a collection of Hui-neng's sermons a "Sútra", a term reserved for the Buddha's own utterances. Because the Ch'an school abhorred all intellectualization and systematizations, its own literature, insofar as it had any, widely departed from the Indian models. A few Ch'an monks seem to have composed sermons and didactic hymns, but the great majority of the T'ang masters refused to write down anything at all. They confined themselves to a few brief and cryptic sayings, which at a later age were collected as "Sayings of the Ancient Worthies". So much did they distrust the distorting effect of words, that they tried to induce enlightenment in their pupils not only by nonsensical remarks, but by beating them at appropriate moments with a stick, pulling their noses, or making rude and inconsequential noises, like Ma-tsu's famous "Ho", etc. Their method of teaching was technically known as "strange words and stranger actions". Because no written work can contain them, these teachings were held to be something outside the scriptures. They are regarded as instances of the "Buddha-mind" speaking directly to the "Buddha-mind", and they transmit the "Seal of Mind" directly from teacher to pupil.

It is, of course, not easy to distil from such unpromising material a rationally formulated philosophical doctrine. But, attempting the impossible, one may well say that these were the chief tenets of Ch'an. First of all, there is the famous teaching that "Buddhahood is achieved through instantaneous enlightenment". As practical people, the Ch'an Buddhists were not, however, so much interested in theories about enlightenment, as in its practical achievement. The Hínayána had much to say about "enlightenment", but could no longer produce any fully enlightened people, be they Arhats or Buddhas. Nor was the traditional Maháyána in any better position and had to justify its apparent sterility by asserting that any given Bodhisattva would have to still pass through aeons and aeons of preparation before he could become a Buddha. In the seventh and eighth centuries a number of Buddhists became rather impatient with doctrines which deferred the attainment of the goal to an indefinite future and insisted on quicker results. This led to the Tantra devising methods for winning Buddhahood "in this very body", and to the Ch'an working for enlightenment "in this very life". The Ch'an claimed that within their ranks numerous people attained "enlightenment" all the time, but for this they did not use the traditional term *p'u-t'i*, which corresponds to *bodhi*, but a new word, *wu*, "comprehension, awareness", better known in its Japanese form as *satori*. Its relation to "enlightenment" in its traditional Indian sense and to the Buddha's omniscience has never to my knowledge been clarified, although the Ch'an Patriarchs are referred to as "venerable Buddhas". This signifies that in the history of Buddhism a new type of "saint" had arisen. After the Arhats, Pratyekabuddhas, Bodhisattvas and Siddhas we now have the Ch'an *Róshis* as a fifth type.

Secondly, the highest principle is inexpressible. Again, Ch'an was not content to just say so, as many Buddhist philosophers had done before them, but it tried to make the insight into this truth into a concrete experience, by evolving methods of "stating it through non-statement", by in other words designing some extraordinary and on the face of it quite irrelevant kind of statement which would do justice to it. Like for instance,

In the square pool there is a turtle-nosed serpent.
Ridiculous indeed when you come to think of it!
Who pulled out the serpent's head?

Analogously, "cultivation must be carried out by non-cultivation". Just as a mirror cannot be made by grinding a brick, so a Buddha cannot be made by practising meditations. This does not mean that all meditation should be discarded, but that it should be carried out without any striving, self-assertion or deliberate purpose, thus exhausting the old karma and creating no new karma. One must be established in "no-thought" which means "to be in thought yet devoid of thought" and to "stop the mind dashing hither and thither". As a result of this kind of cultivation, a man gains enlightenment, he has no more doubts and all his problems are suddenly solved, not because he has found a solution for them, but because they have ceased to be problems for him. And although his new-found knowledge is different from the ignorance of ordinary people, nevertheless, in the last resort, he has gained nothing at all, and the life of the sage is not different from that of ordinary men. As Yi-hsuan (died 867) put it: "Only do ordinary things with no special effort: relieve your bowels, pass water, wear your clothes, eat your food, and, when tired, lie down! Simple fellows will laugh at you, but the wise will understand." So "there is really nothing much in the Buddhist teaching". The secret which the Buddha gave to Mahákásyapa is really an open secret, and there is nothing to it, except that the mass of people fail to understand it.

Once enlightened, the sage can without any effort combine a mysterious aloofness with a constant response to the calls of the world. Non-activity has become identical with action, and, as P'ang-yun put it, "spirit-like understanding and divine functioning lies in carrying water and chopping wood". To conclude with a saying of Hai-yun: "To eat all day yet not to swallow a grain of rice; to walk all day yet not tread an inch of ground; to have no distinction during that time between object and subject, and to be inseparable from things all day long, yet not be deluded by them, this is to be the man who is at ease in himself." Ch'an is a very profound doctrine indeed. Although the cultural background and social conditions of the China of the T'ang differed in almost every way from those of the India of the Buddha Śākyamuni, rarely have Buddhists at any time come as near to the spirit of their Founder as the great masters of the Ch'an school.

So far about the intellectual developments of the period. Outwardly also under the T'ang the Buddhist Church attained a position of greater brilliance, wealth and power than it has probably experienced at any other time during its long history. This success was, however, bought at a heavy price. The prosperity of the monasteries threatened to ruin the economy of the country. The vast monastic establishments were economically unproductive, and had to be maintained by the lay community, i.e. by the Imperial Court, by aristocratic families or by villages; the expensive architectural enterprises deflected huge numbers of the rural population from work in the fields, and finally the metallic reserves of the country were drained away, being used to cast images and other ritual objects. This process led to the great persecution of 845. The Government confiscated the property of the monasteries, forced the monks and nuns to return to secular life, and seized the works of art in order to use the metal for more secular purposes.

Buddhism came to *Korea* officially in AD 372, and by about 525 it had penetrated the entire country. Between 550 and 664 it became the state religion and steadily grew in power, with the monks periodically dominating the rulers. Kings, princes and princesses often became bonzes and everywhere magnificent temples, statues and other monuments were erected. There were no notable developments in doctrine. Korean Buddhism was chiefly significant by acting as an intermediary between China and Japan. Apart from that it was noteworthy for the fervour with which it was practised, and for centuries all the surplus wealth of the country was expended on religious purposes.

7 JAPAN

About 550 Buddhism came to Japan from Korea, as one of the constituent elements of Chinese civilization and a great statesman, Shotoku Taishi (523–621), adopted it as a kind of religion. Soon it fused with the indigenous Shintó which had at first fiercely opposed it. At first it was said, as in Tibet of the indigenous deities, that the Shintó gods are the guardians and protectors of Buddhism. Then the pantheon of the two schools was slowly identified and it was taught that they were just the same deities under different names. In the ninth century this amalgamation received the name of Ryóbu-Shintó. The Ryóbu Shintó is a remarkable achievement not only for the reason that it effectively fused the two religions for the time being, but also because it fused them in such a way that 1,000 years later it was quite easy to separate them again.

This was a period of copying. Before 700 four "sects" were introduced, which were not however corporations pledged to support particular doctrines, but simply philosophical schools which expounded certain textbooks. They were the *Jójitsu* (625) based on Kumárajíva's translation of Harivarman's "Satyasiddhi"; the *Sanron* (625) which studied the three works of Nágárjuna and Áryadeva which were the basis of the Chinese San-lun school; the *Hossó* (654) which has for its textbook the Yuishiki, which expounds the principles of Vijñánaváda after Yüan-tsang and K'uei-ki; and the *Kusha* (658) which was devoted to the exposition of Vasubandhu's Abhidharmakośa. Then came the Hua-yen (730), now called

Kegon, which lasted for many centuries, and worshipped Vairocana, as Roshana or Birushana; and also the Vinaya sect (753) which was called *Risshú* tried to introduce stricter rules of ordination, and declined soon.

Much more substantial were the sects introduced during the Heian period (794–1186), which was dominated by the *Tendai* and *Shingon* who had their centres on two mountains. The one was founded by Dengyó Daishi (767–822) who had brought the T'ien-t'ai doctrine from China, the other by Kóbó Daishi (774–835) who had learned the mysteries of the Chén-yen in Chang-an. The sacred Tendai mountains of Hieizan near the new capital of Kyótó were soon covered by no fewer than 3,000 temples or halls. The Tendai not only had a great influence on art, but all later sects arose from within it, in the sense that their founders had for a time belonged to this sect. Kóbó Daishi on his return from China not only became a great favourite at the imperial court, but he also impressed the popular imagination more than any other Japanese teacher has done. For the people he is the hero of countless legends, for his followers a manifestation of Vairocana not yet dead, but awaiting within his tomb the coming of the future Buddha.

The centre of the Shingon sect was on the lonely mountain of Kóyasan, and the performance of ritual has been its main activity, apart from the execution of paintings and sculptures of Tantric deities. Not all the monks of Tendai and Shingon resided in monasteries, and there was a strong movement within both schools to revive the ardours of the early Buddhist community, when the monks actually dwelled in the forest. There was a considerable number of Yama-bushi, "those who sleep on mountains", or Shugenja, "those who practise austerities", who lived alone or in little groups in the wild mountains and forests. On the whole, both Tendai and Shingon chiefly addressed themselves to the educated classes and their popular appeal was not very strong. To those who desired an easier way they held out the invocation of Amida's name which would lead to rebirth in the Western Paradise. Both the Nara and Heian sects built special halls for recitation of the *Nembutsu*, accompanied by hymns and musical services. At the same time during the tenth century itinerant preachers brought the message of Amida's saving grace to the masses in a language which they could understand.

Buddhism took on the colouring of the social conditions in which it lived. The esteem in which the religion was held was to a large extent a tribute to its beneficial magical effects on the welfare of the nation. Monasteries were by their very presence preserved from the noxious influences which arise out of the earth in certain places, and the recital of the great Maháyána Sútras was regularly carried out for the purpose of averting plagues, earthquakes, and other disasters. The moral precepts, on the other hand, were not always closely observed. In the Heian period there were violent quarrels between the monasteries, who had become huge territorial magnates, and behaved as feudal institutions usually do. Organized bodies of mercenaries commanded by priests burned down each other's monasteries, and appeared in armed bands in Kyoto to force the hands of the government. Aesthetic culture was the chief note of the age, and much of its wonderful art has survived.

8 TIBET

In Tibet Buddhism is said to have begun about 650, but it made real headway only a century later. At first it met with fierce resistance from the shamans of the native Bon religion, who had the support of the greater part of the nobility. The patronage of the king, however, enabled the Buddhists gradually to establish themselves, and under King Ral-pa-can (817–36) they reached the height of their influence. In 787 the first monastery was completed at bSam Yas and soon after the first monks were ordained by Śántarakshita. Everywhere temples were erected, many teachers invited from India, a script was invented and numerous works were translated. Great endeavours were made to ensure the accuracy of the translations and the terminology was standardized about 825 by a commission consisting of Indian pandits and Tibetan Lotsabas, which published the *Mahávyutpatti* for the guidance of translators. The Bon rivals seemed defeated, the monks seized the effective rule of the country, but then under gLang-dar-ma (836–42) a persecution wiped out everything that had been gained. For about one century Buddhism once more vanished from Tibet.

The period under review is for Tibet one of reception. In the course of it four principal systems, or lines of thought, were introduced:

1. From the West, from the Swat valley, came the Tantric ideas of *Padmasambhava*, who himself stayed in Tibet for a short while. Padmasambhava's mentality had considerable affinities with that of the Bon and he had a striking success in Tibet. He expounded some kind of Vajrayánic system, but we do not know exactly which one. The impression he made on Tibet was chiefly based on his thaumaturgical activities and the legend has quite overgrown the historical facts. The school of the *Nyingmapa*, or "Ancient Ones", goes back to Padmasambhava and has persisted continuously up to today.

2. From the South came the *Pála Synthesis* of the Maháyána, brought by some of the leading scholars of the universities of Magadha. This combination of Prajñápáramitá and Tantra has become the central tradition of Tibetan Buddhism,

and has renewed itself again and again up to the present day. It has always attached a special value to the *Abhisamayálankára*, an Indian work of the fourth century, which arranges the contents of the "Prajñápáramitá in 25,000 Slokas" in definite numerical lists, that make it possible to memorize the text as a preliminary step to meditation on it, while at the same time interpreting it in the spirit of the Mádhyamikas with some admixture from the more moderate Yogácárin tradition. Frequently commented upon already in India, the Abhisamayálankára now in Tibet became the cornerstone of the more advanced non-Tantric training and innumerable commentaries have been composed on it by the learned men of Tibet.

3. Thirdly, from the South-West the *Sarvástivádins* also attempted to gain a foothold in Tibet. Quite early on the king invited them to establish a monastery, but their settlements soon withered away, the surrounding population remaining indifferent to a teaching which lacked in magical practices. Although they could not maintain themselves for long in this world of magic and witchcraft, the Sarvástivádins have nevertheless exerted a considerable influence on the thought of Tibet, because their literature is practically the only version of the older type of Buddhism to find its way into the Canon of translated scriptures.

4. The fourth influence came from the East. Numerous Chinese monks of the *Ch'an Sect* appeared in Tibet and attempted to convert its inhabitants to their tenets. They soon came into conflict with the Indian pandits of the Pála orthodoxy, and were decisively defeated at the famous Council of bSam Yas in 793–4. After that they had to leave the country, or go underground, and their influence on later Tibetan history is negligible.

CHAPTER

4

THE
LAST ONE THOUSAND YEARS
AD 1000–1978

1 INDIA: THE COLLAPSE AND ITS CAUSES

In India itself, Buddhism came to an end about 1200, though in some districts, as in Magadha, Bengal, Orissa and South India, it lingered on for a further 200 or 300 years.

The main cause which precipitated its disappearance was, of course, the Mohammedan invasions. In their fanatical hatred for what seemed to them 'idolatry', these ruthless conquerors burned down the flourishing monasteries and universities of Sind and Bengal, and killed the monks, who offered no resistance, partly in obedience to their vows, and partly because they believed that astrological calculations had shown that the Muslims would in any case conquer Hindustan. On further consideration Muslim savagery cannot, however, be the whole explanation and that for two reasons: Firstly, Hinduism and Jainism, subjected to the same fury, managed to carry on. Secondly, in regions which were not touched by the Muslim invasions, as in Nepal and South India, Buddhism also steadily died out, though much more slowly. Hence the cause of this decline must be sought as much within Buddhism as without it.

As a *social force* an unworldly religion can only survive if by some accident it is able to enlist the support of some powerful or wealthy section of society. If the Jains alone among the numerous ancient sects of India are still a power in that country, it is because by some accident wealthy merchants are numbered among its adherents, merchants who regard it as an honour to support the ascetics. Buddhism has generally relied on the support of kings and where that was wanting it has usually been in difficulties. It has, as we saw (p. 34), never succeeded in doing very much for the average lay follower, and therefore the monks cannot normally live on their voluntary patronage. The Buddhist laity never formed a corporate social entity, or a homogenous group living apart from the followers of the Brahminical sects, and it had throughout conformed to the Brahminical caste system and followed Brahminical rites in ceremonies at birth, marriage, and death. So any weakening of the monasteries would automatically lead to the absorption of the lay followers into the closely knit social structure of Brahminism. The Jains survived because a living community existed between monks and laymen, but the Buddhists were lacking in that. The international character of Buddhism, which had enabled it to conquer Asia, also favoured its extinction in India. The Buddhist religion had always inculcated indifference to the particular country in which the monks were living, and so the surviving monks left the country in which they could no longer practise their monastic rules, and went to Nepal, Tibet, China, etc. Their less flexible and more earthbound Hindu and Jain brethren stood their ground, and in the end they survived where they were.

As a *spiritual force* Buddhism had played itself out. There is no reason to believe that after 1,000 the Buddhist monks were any lazier or more corrupt than at any time, and in any case the history of religion knows numerous cases where corruption has been healed by reformation. In fact, when we see the calibre of the men whom the Indian foundations could still send to Tibet, it is difficult to believe in their depravity or degeneracy. But what had ceased was the creative impulse. The Buddhists had nothing new to say any more. By analogy with what happened in the first and sixth centuries, a new outburst of creative activity was due in the eleventh, and was necessary to the rejuvenation of the religion. It failed to take place.

What had of course happened was that in the course of 1,700 years of co-existence the Hindus had taken over a great deal from the Buddhists and the Buddhists likewise from the Hindus. In consequence the division between them had increasingly diminished and it was no great thing for a Buddhist to be absorbed into the largely Buddhified Hindu fold. The Buddha and some Buddhist deities were incorporated into the Hindu pantheon. The philosophy of Nágárjuna had been absorbed into the Vedánta by Gaudapáda, Śánkara's teacher, just as the Vaishnavas of later times were greatly indebted to the Buddhists. The Buddhist Tantras had provoked their Hindu counterparts, which abound with references to Maháyána deities. There had been a constant assimilation in the iconography and mythology of the two religions. It is a law of history that the co-existence of rival views must lead to some form of eclecticism. This is merely the reproduction of the effects of osmotic pressure in the intellectual field. So it was in the Greco-Roman world with the philosophical systems, and so with the political parties in England in the fifties, their main difficulty being to find something to disagree on. The same happened to Hinduism and Buddhism. The separate existence of Buddhism no longer served a useful purpose. Its disappearance thus was no loss to anyone. We must also not forget the Buddhist conviction that this is a period of religious decline. In Orissa the Buddhists said that in the inauspicious Kali Yuga the Buddhists must disguise themselves and worship Hari, waiting patiently for the time when the Buddhas will reappear.

Hostile critics generally scrutinize the collapse of Buddhism in India on the assumption that there must have been something wrong with it. "It is always so easy to flog a dead horse", as one of these historians himself admits, and Darwinian preconceptions about the "survival of the fittest" may mislead when applied to religions. Everything has its duration, its allotted life-span — trees, animals, nations, social institutions, and religions are no exception. What Buddhism in India died from was just old age, or sheer exhaustion. Nor had it ever believed that it was exempt from the impermanence of all conditioned things which it had preached so often. In fact, in their wisdom, its teachers had foreseen the coming end. For centuries the fall of the Order had been predicted for a period about 1,500 years after the Buddha's Nirvana and Yüan-tsang not only recounts many legends current in many places in India in the seventh century which showed an expectation of the coming end, but he himself had, amidst the grandeurs of Nálandá, a dream to the effect that fire would devastate this celebrated centre of learning, and that its halls would one day be deserted. So when the end came it was in no way unexpected and all that was left was to disappear gracefully from the scene.

2 NEPAL AND KASHMIR

The Moslem persecutions induced many monks and scholars of Northern India to flee to Nepal, bringing their books and holy images with them. Nepal thus became a repository of Pála Buddhism. Nevertheless even the arrival of the refugees from India failed to infuse new vigour into the Buddhism of Nepal, and after AD 1000 it presents a picture of increasing decay. Royal patronage kept the Samgha alive for some time, and for a few centuries the country remained a centre of Buddhist culture.

Scholars can determine the extent of the decadence by the condition of the Sanskrit manuscripts. These are very good about AD 1200, they become fair in the seventeenth century, and in the nineteenth they become so careless and slovenly that little reliance can be placed on them. Likewise the quality of the art goes steadily down and down. With the collapse of Buddhism in India the Buddhists of Nepal had to rely on their own strength. Reduced to one small valley, they capitulated to Hinduism within a hundred years or so. In the course of the fourteenth century the monks decided that the monastic rules were too difficult to keep, and they transformed themselves into a Hindu caste, calling themselves the *banras* ("honourable ones"). They gave up their celibacy, moved into the *viháras* with their families, and have ever since continued to earn their living as metal workers. Deprived of its elite, Nepalese Buddhism could only preserve some of the outward forms of the religion. A number of deities are worshipped in the manner of Hindu gods and for centuries lay Buddhism alone has prevailed in Nepal. The most popular deities are Matsyendranáth, "Lord Indra of the Fish", a deified Yogin, identified with Lokeśvara, and also Tárá, the "Saviouress", who, however, as the centuries passed on, has lost ground to the Śivaite Kálí.

In the popular cult the dividing lines from Hinduism have become more and more blurred. In some cases the same image does service for both, e.g. the Hindu looks upon Mahákála as Śiva or Vishnu, the Buddhist as Vajrapáni; or Hindu pilgrims at Tundiktel worship the guardian deity of Nepal, Buddhists the same image as Padmapáni.

Not that all scholarship and intellectual life has been completely extinct. Hodgson, the British Resident, tells us that early in the nineteenth century there were four philosophical schools, called the Svábhávikas, Aiśvarikas, Kármikas and

Yátnikas. But, like so many other English Proconsuls, he had no taste for philosophy, refused to be drawn into "the interminable absurdities of the Bauddha system", and his account of their differences gives little sense. Curiously enough, no one since has tried to determine the points in dispute. The conquest of the country by the Gurkhas in 1768 reduced the Buddhist Newars to the status of a subject race, and that was the final blow which further accelerated the decay which was the inevitable consequence of the disappearance of the Samgha of homeless monks. In recent years missionaries from both Ceylon and Tibet have attempted to found a new Samgha in Nepal, and any revival of the religion will depend on the success of their endeavours.

In Kashmir, the last centuries of Hindu rule were on the whole years of misrule, and the years between 855 and 1338 represent a period of continuous decline and of political disintegration. Buddhism and Śivaism fused and Buddhists and Śivaites often lived together in the same religious foundations. After 1000, many Kashmiri scholars and craftsmen went to Tibet, Ladakh, Guge and Spiti, and between 1204–13 Śákyasríbhadra, "the Great Kashmiri Scholar" was prominent in Tibet. The year 1339 marked the beginning of Muslim rule. At first that was tolerant to the Buddhists, but about 1400 the persecution began in earnest, images, temples and monasteries were systematically destroyed, religious ceremonies and processions were forbidden, and about 1500 Buddhism came to an end as a distinct faith, not without leaving strong traces on the Hinduism in that region and fainter traces even on the Muslims. For the rest everything was totally wrecked.

3 CEYLON

In 1160 a council at Anurádhapura terminated the dissensions between the Mahávihára and its rivals by the suppression of the latter. Soon after 1200 there was a collapse, not so much of Buddhism, as of the social system which supported it. Invasions from India weakened the central power, which could no longer enforce the irrigation works and soon Muslim pirates and even Chinese eunuchs ruled over large stretches of the land. The economic basis of the Samgha in this way became extremely precarious. Later on, beginning in the sixteenth century, the Portuguese persecuted Buddhism, claimed to have destroyed the Sacred Tooth, and forced many Ceylonese to become Roman Catholics. Then followed the Dutch, and finally the English (until 1948). The long centuries of European rule did great harm to the Buddhist cause. The Samgha often died out completely, and monks had to be repeatedly imported from Burma and Siam, in the seventeenth, eighteenth and nineteenth centuries. The revival began about 1880, first stimulated by the Theosophical Society, and then carried out under the impulse of awakening nationalism. Since that time Ceylonese Buddhists have become increasingly active and have done a great deal of valuable scholarly work, though generally within the limits of a rather narrow orthodoxy, and in 1950 they took the lead in trying to bring all Buddhist countries together, and set up the World Fellowship of Buddhists.

4 SOUTH-EAST ASIA

At the beginning of this period the Buddhism of *Burma* changes its character, and draws its inspiration henceforth from Ceylon. In 1057 King Anawrahta of Págan conquers Thaton to take possession of the Páli Tipitaka and the relics stored there. He then has monks and scriptures brought from Ceylon, and the chronicles assure us that he "drove out" the Ari priests of the Vajrayána. There is, however, much evidence for the persistence of the Maháyána after that date. Archaeology has shown that it was during the suzerainty of the Anawrahta dynasty (1044–1283) that the Maháyána flourished most, side by side with the more popular Theraváda. Many sculptures of Maháyána deities date back to that time, Maháyána texts were found in the monasteries up to the fifteenth century, and unmistakably Tantric paintings can still be seen on the walls of temples near Págan, first in the style of Bengal, and later in that of Nepal. The Aris were certainly abhorrent to the Theravádins, because they ate meat, drank spirits, used spells to remove guilt, practised animal sacrifices and indulged in erotic practices, but nevertheless they continued to exist until the end of the eighteenth century.

The patronage of the Court went, however, to the Theravádins, and Págan, until its destruction by the Mongols in 1287, was a great centre of Buddhist culture, and witnessed during three centuries one of those outbursts of devotion of which we have seen other examples in China, Korea, and Tibet. For eight miles the land was filled with 9,000 pagodas and temples, among which the most famous is the Ananda temple of the eleventh century. The 547 Játaka stories are here represented on glazed plaques.

After the collapse of the central dynasty Burma was for 500 years divided into warring kingdoms, but the Theraváda tradition continued, though less splendidly than before. The end of the fifteenth century saw the final triumph of the Sinhalese school, when king Dhammaceti of Pegu reintroduced a canonically valid monastic succession from Ceylon. In 1752 Burma was united again, after 1852 the dynasty vigorously patronized the Samgha and a Council at Mandalay in 1868–71 corrected the text of the Tipitaka, which was then incised on 729 marble slabs. The coming of the English in 1885 did much harm to the Samgha by destroying the central ecclesiastical authority. In the struggle for independence the monks played a prominent part. During recent years attempts have been made to combine Buddhism with Marxism, and also a new method of meditation has been advocated which by employing Tantric practices is said to lead to speedier results.

Burmese Buddhism is bent on preserving Theravāda orthodoxy and it has made no creative contribution to Buddhist thought. Disputes have always been confined to the externalities of the Vinaya and the extensive literature consists of works on grammar, astrology and medicine, of commentaries and of adaptations of Jātakas. The thirty-seven *Nats*, or "spirits", are universally asked for their favours, but the chief means of acquiring merit is to build a pagoda, with the result that the country is covered with them. The Samgha is not estranged from the people, monasteries and shrines are placed near the centres of habitation, so as to be easily accessible to laymen, every layman becomes a novice for a time, and receives some education in the monasteries. The population, 85 per cent Buddhist, has been distinguished by its high degree of literacy for a long time. Buddhism has been a great civilizing force in the life of Burma, has helped to tone down racial rivalries, fostered a democratic social life by minimizing the importance of wealth and caste, brought much beauty and knowledge with it, and above all, it has created a singularly cheerful, polite and likeable people.

Theravāda Buddhism during our period likewise took over in *Thailand* and Indo-China. The Thais brought from their home in China some form of Buddhism, but in the fourteenth century the Ceylonese Theravāda was established. The capitals – first Ayuthia (1330–1767) and then Bangkok (after 1770) – are large, magnificent Buddhist cities with immense religious edifices and great Buddhas. Buddhism is the state religion, all indigenous culture is bound up with it and the king is the "Protector of Dhamma" not only in word but also in deed. Tradition is strictly followed and the rhythmical recitation of Páli texts is greatly stressed. Petitions, as in Burma, are not directed to the Buddha but to local genii and tree spirits.

Whereas in the eleventh century the Tantrayána still flourished in *Cambodia*, after 1300 the Theraváda as a result of the Thai pressure slowly replaced it and in the fifteenth century the Ceylonese orthodoxy was imported. Also here the education is in the hands of the monks and Buddhism has proved itself an elevating and ennobling influence, and has produced a mild, kindly and helpful people. The *Neaca-ta*, or spirits of the land, also play their part and there is some blending of influences from China (e.g. the presence of Mi-lei-fo in the temples) and from India (e.g. the Nágas, Garudas and four-faced Śivas found in architecture). The history of Buddhism in *Laos* is shrouded in legend. It seems to have been introduced in the fourteenth century by Khmer immigrants, and at present is of the Siamese type, with greater emphasis on the Nágas. *Annam* finally, independent since 1000, is culturally a part of China, and the Maháyána has existed there for a long time.

In *Indonesia* Tantric Buddhism persisted until it was suppressed by Islam, in Sumatra at the end of the fourteenth century, in Java from the fifteenth century onwards. Its final collapse was preceded by a slow decline in the Hindu impact on the culture and a re-assertion of the more indigenous elements. The Tantrism prevalent in this period was an extremist form, which enjoined the practice of the five makáras, "free from all sensualities", and regarded Vairocana as the primordial Buddha. It syncretized the Kálacakra with the devotion to Śiva Bhairava into a cult of *Śiva-buddha* and, in keeping with the native Indonesian tradition, it was chiefly devoted to the redemption of the souls of the dead. Some of the loveliest pieces of Buddhist sculpture were made in Java under the dynasty of Singhasari (1222–92), which represented its kings on statues as Amoghapáśa, Aksobhya, etc., and its queens as Prajñápáramitá, etc.

5 CHINA AND KOREA

Although the Sung emperors were on the whole well disposed towards Buddhism, its vigour declined during this period. After about AD 1000 two schools ousted all the others, the Amidism of Faith, and the meditational school of Ch'an. Within Ch'an, five lines of transmission, called the "Five Houses", had taken shape. All Ch'an Buddhists alike believe that one's own heart is the Buddha, but there are obviously great differences in the hearts of men and these must inevitably reflect themselves in different methods and approaches. What therefore differentiated the "Five Houses" were less differences in doctrine than differences in style. Three of the five, the *Wei-yang-tsung*, the *Yün-men-tsung* and the *Fa-yen-tsung*, died out already by the middle of the Sung period. Characteristic of the Wei-yang sect was a special method of teaching by drawing various circles in the air or on the ground; the Yün-men sect generally resembled the Lin-chi, but one of its special devices was the reply to questions with one single word of one syllable; the Fa-yen was more favourable to the study of the Sútras than the other Ch'an sects and the influence on it of the Hua-yen doctrines was particularly marked.

The two schools which have survived to the present day are the *Ts'ao-tung-tsung*, founded by Tung-shan Liang-chieh (807–69), and the *Lin-chi-tsung*, which goes back to his contemporary Lin-chi-I-hsüan (died 867). The differences between these two, which had been just distinctive tendencies

117

so far, hardened into different sects in the proper sense of the term only about 1150. The Ts'ao-tung was always characterized by quietism and Hung-chih Cheng-chüeh (died 1157) gave it the special name of *Mo-chao ch'an* "silent-illumination Ch'an". This indicated that the school stressed the quiet sitting still in silent meditation, by or in which enlightenment, or spiritual insight into absolute emptiness, is attained. The founder of this sect was mild and gentle in his methods. He also bequeathed to his school a special doctrine concerning the "Five Ranks", which distinguishes five stages of the movement towards enlightenment in a thoroughly Chinese manner which was greatly indebted to the Book of Changes, and the stages were represented by white and black circles. Four doctrines are mentioned as characteristic of the Ts'ao-tung: (1) All beings have the Buddha-nature at birth and consequently are essentially enlightened; (2) They can enjoy fully the Bliss of the Buddha-nature while in a state of quiet meditation; (3) Practice and knowledge must always complement one another; (4) The strict observance of religious ritual must be carried over into our daily lives. The founder of the Lin-chi sect by contrast favoured the use of rudeness and abruptness and the "shout and the stick" played a great part in the practices of this school. It was the most hostile of them all to rationalization and the most emphatic in stressing the suddenness and directness of Ch'an experience.

During the Sung the Ch'an school became a cultural factor of great importance. Many Ch'an monks were found among the painters of the period, and its influence on art was considerable. Even the Neo-Confucian Renaissance of Chu-hsi and others owed much to Ch'an Buddhism, just as the Vedantic Renaissance of Śankara had been greatly indebted to Maháyána Buddhism. The practice of *tso-ch'an*, quiet contemplation, so

important in Ch'an, found its way into the practices of
Confucianism as *ching-tso*, or "quiet-sitting". This outward
success brought its dangers and led to a deep crisis within
Ch'an. The T'ang masters had always avoided the capital, but
now the Ch'an monasteries maintained excellent relations with
the Court and meddled much in politics. Magnificent Ch'an
monasteries arose throughout the country and became focal
points of social and cultural life. Many concessions were made
to intellectualism and to the study of the Sútras, and within the
Ch'an camp a vigorous controversy arose about their
importance.

Most radical in its rejection of the authority of the Sútras
was the Lin-chi, which countered the impending decadence by
evolving the *kung-an* system. The word *Kung-an* consists of two
characters, for "government" and "legal case" and denotes a
precedent or authoritative model. In practice a *kung-an* is a
riddle, usually connected with a saying or action of one of the
T'ang masters. Collections of such *kung-ans* were now published
and to each was added an explanation which deliberately never
explained anything at all. The first example of this new literary
genre was a collection of 100 riddles, called the *Pi-yen-lu*,
which appeared in 1125. The other famous collection is the
"Gateless Gate", or *Wu-men-kuan*, comprising 48 cases, and
which appeared more than a century later. In opposition to the
quietism advocated by the Ts'ao-tung, the Lin-chi advocated
ceaseless activity on the chosen *kung-an* which must be carried
on until sudden enlightenment supervenes. As Ta-hui tsung-kao
(1089–1163) put it: "Just steadily go on with your *kung-an* every
moment of your life! Whether walking or sitting, let your
attention be fixed upon it without interruption. When you
begin to find it entirely devoid of flavour, the final moment is
approaching: do not let it slip out of your grasp! When all of a

119

sudden something flashes out in your mind, its light will illuminate the entire universe, and you will see the spiritual land of the Enlightened Ones fully revealed at the point of a single hair and the wheel of the Dharma revolving in a single grain of dust." In Sung times systematic method thus replaced the individualistic spontaneity of the T'ang masters. But it was this systematization and to some extent mechanization which assured the survival of Ch'an.

Whenever philosophical schools coexist for any length of time, the result will be an increasing syncretism between them. In many ways Ch'an was combined with Huayen and T'ien-t'ai, and the practice of the *Nembutsu* was often brought in to strengthen the Ch'an meditation. During the Yüan and Ming dynasties a fairly complete fusion of the different trends of Chinese Buddhism actually took place. The Ming and Manchus favoured Confucianism, but tolerated, and occasionally encouraged Buddhism. Two emperors, Yung-cheng (1723–35) and Ch'ien-lung (1736–95), tried to create a type of Buddhism which combined Chinese Buddhist (Fo-ist) and Lamaist elements, thus appealing to Chinese on the one hand, and Tibetans and Mongols on the other. The Yung-ho-kung, the Lamaist Cathedral in Peking, is a visible monument to these endeavours and in it the deities proper to these two types of Buddhist cult are carefully blended. Even Kuan Ti, the Chinese War God, and Confucius are there enlisted among the Bodhisattvas. The prosperity of the monasteries has never recovered from the Taiping rebellion of the "long-haired Christians", who for fifteen years (1850–65) devastated sixteen provinces, destroyed 600 cities, and thousands of temples and monasteries. Nevertheless, until the present day Buddhism has remained a by no means negligible factor in the cultural and religious life of China.

In *Korea*, Buddhism reached the height of its power under the Koryo dynasty, particularly between 1140 and 1390. The founder of the dynasty was a pious Buddhist, who attributed his success to the Buddha's protection. His successors never wavered in their support of the religion. Each king chose a bonze as his "preceptor", or advisor. The holy scriptures were carried in front of the kings when they travelled. Fine editions of the Canon were printed at the expense of the state, one of them comprising 81,258 leaves. For long stretches of time the government was entirely in the hands of the bonzes. Up to the twelfth century the aristocracy had been the main support of Buddhism, but now it became the religion of the common people as well. Strong magical elements entered into Buddhism, as has happened to this religion wherever it became really popular. Many bonzes became experts in prolonging life, in working miracles, evoking spirits, distinguishing between auspicious and inauspicious times and places, and so on. In 1036 an edict abolished the death penalty and decreed that out of four sons one must become a monk. The Koryo dynasty expended much wealth on magnificent religious ceremonies and buildings, and innumerable works of art were created under it. During the Yüan dynasty, especially after 1258, Lamaism exerted a considerable influence. In the fourteenth century the Buddhists dominated Korea almost completely. In 1310 it was decreed that the monks need not salute anyone whereas everyone else must show respect to them. Those who had chosen the religious life were exempt from all material cares.

The excessively privileged position of the church came to an abrupt end with the change of the dynasty in 1392. Confucianism now gained the upper hand, the monks were deprived of official support and a share in political life, their lands were confiscated, they were forbidden to pray at funerals, the twenty-three convents existing in Seoul were closed, and Buddhism was generally discouraged. As a religion of the masses it nevertheless persisted, away from the cities, in the rather inaccessible Diamond Mountains. Doctrinally, this Buddhism was the usual Chinese mixture of Ch'an, Amidism and local superstitions. Between 1910 and 1945 the Japanese fostered Buddhism, but it remained in a rather debilitated condition. In 1947, about 7,000 monks were counted in Korea.

6 JAPAN

During this period a second flowering of Buddhism took place in Japan. Between 1160 and 1260 new sects arose which entirely changed its character, and Japanese Buddhism now reached the height of its originality and creative power. In the Kamakura period (1192–1335) the Amida schools and Zen came into the foreground, just as they did in China after AD 1000.

The first *Amida* sect, known as the Yúzú Nembutsu, was founded already in 1124 by Ryónin, who saw the way to salvation in the constant recitation of the "Nembutsu", i.e. of the formula *Namu Amida Butsu*, up to 60,000 times a day. He also taught that this invocation was infinitely more meritorious if repeated on behalf of others than for one's own selfish ends. His sect, though still in existence, never commanded a large following. Far more influential was the Jódó, or "Pure Land", school, founded by Hónen (1133–1212), an exceptionally learned and gentle priest. In 1175, at the age of 43, Shan-tao's works led him to the conclusion that the traditional Buddhist moral and mental disciplines were no longer effective in this age of decay. Whatever in such an age we may do by our own efforts (*jiriki*) is of no avail. Peace can only be found through the strength of another (*tariki*), in self-surrender and in reliance on a higher power, that of the Buddha Amitábha. Hónen therefore abandoned all other religious practices, and devoted himself exclusively to the recitation of Amida's name. All that matters is to "repeat the name of Amida with all your heart – whether walking or standing still, whether sitting or lying, never cease to practise it for even a moment!" In these evil days the only way to obtain salvation is to strive to be reborn in Amida's "Western Paradise" (Jó-dó), and the "holy path" (shó-dó), consisting of good works and religious exercises, no longer works. A simple faith in Amida is all that is needed. It will carry even the greatest sinner into Amida's Blessed Land. Hónen drew, however, no antinomian inferences from this assertion and enjoined his followers to avoid sin, to observe the monastic regulations, and also to show no disrespect to the other Buddhas and to the Sútras. His teaching had an instantaneous success at the Court, among the aristocracy, the Samurai and the clergy, and the new movement maintained itself easily against the hostility of the older sects. The Jódó school has continued to the present day without much modification. But in the fourteenth century the seventh patriarch Ryóyó Shógei made an interesting and influential re-interpretation. Rebirth in the Pure Land, so he said, does not mean that one is transported into another region, but the Pure Land is everywhere, and to go there is a change of mind and condition, and not of place. This is very much in agreement with the tradition of Maháyána.

A further simplification of Amidism was effected by Shinran (born 1173), one of Hónen's disciples, and the founder of the *Shin* sect, the word *shin* being an abbreviation of Jódó Shinshú, "the True Jódó Sect". Shinran broke with the monastic traditions, got married and advised his followers to do likewise. He regarded the constant repetition of the *Nembutsu* as unnecessary, and asserted that to call on Amida once only with a believing mind was sufficient to secure birth in His Paradise. The faith in Amida is, however, Amida's own free gift. As to the problem of morality, Shinran maintained that a wicked man is more likely to get into Amida's Land than a good man, because he is less likely to trust in his own strength and merits. The clergy of this sect disclaimed all learning, but as the teachings lend themselves to misunderstanding, great theological subtleties were evolved in the course of time. The devotional practices of this and other Amida schools led to the multiplication of images of Amida, to whom also hymns (*wasan*) in Japanese were written. Shinran aimed at breaking down the barriers between religion and the common people, and in fact the Shinshū became one of the most popular sects and has remained so to the present day.

Less successful was the third Amidist sect, founded by Ippen in 1276, and called the *Ji*, or "the Time", to indicate that it was the proper religion for these degenerate times. In the tradition of the Ryóbu-Shintó he identified a number of Shintó deities with Amida, but as for the *Nembutsu* Ippen even regarded faith as unnecessary, for is it not an activity of the corrupt human mind? The recitation of Amida's name is effective as a result of the sound alone, *ex opere operato*, as it were.

The fourth devotionalist sect, founded in 1253 by Nichiren, the son of a fisherman, differs from all other Buddhist schools by its nationalistic, pugnacious and intolerant attitude and it is somewhat doubtful whether it belongs to the history of Buddhism at all. The patriotic fervour of Nichiren is accounted for by the fact that nationalist sentiments had at that time been greatly inflamed by the long-standing threat of Mongol invasion, which was finally dispelled by the repulsion of Khubilai's armadas in 1274 and

1281. Nichiren replaced the *Nembutsu* with the formula *Namu Myōhō Renge-kyō*, "Homage to the Sútra of the Lotus of the Good Law", and declared that this phrase alone was suitable for this, the last period of Buddhism, which is that of *mappó*, "the destruction of the Law", and which according to him began about AD 1050. Nichiren always spoke with the vehemence of a Hebrew prophet and demanded the suppression of all sects except his own. "For the Nembutsu is hell; the Zen are devils; Shingon is a national ruin, and the Risshú are traitors to the country." On this occasion Buddhism had evolved its very antithesis out of itself.

As for the *Zen* school, Eisai (1141–1215) introduced the Lin-chi sect into Japan, where it became known as *Rinzai*, and attained a great success, whereas the Ts'ao-tung, or *Sóto*, was first introduced by Dógen (1200–33), and then organized and popularized by Keizan Jokin (1268–1325). Dógen's principal work, "The Eye of the True Law", was written in Japanese, so that all could read it. He insisted that, although his generation clearly belonged to the decline of Buddhism, this was no reason for heroic spirits to aim at less than insight into the highest Truth. Against the intellectualist distortions of Buddhism he maintained that "attainment of the Way can only be achieved with one's body". *Zazen*, or "sitting cross-legged", is not a set of meditational practices in which one waits for enlightenment to come, but enlightenment is an inherent principle of Zen meditation from the outset, and it should be carried out as an absolutely pure religious exercise from which nothing is sought and nothing is gained. Everything is the Buddha-nature, and that in its turn is nothing more than "the chin of the donkey or the mouth of a horse". The Sótó sect claims that in Japan it went beyond the developments the parent sect had reached in China, and it gives as an instance of this its belief that, because man is already enlightened from birth, all daily activities should be regarded as post-enlightenment exercises, which should be performed as acts of gratitude to the Buddha (*gyojiho-on*).

Zen soon spread among the Samurai, particularly in its Rinzai form, in accordance with the proverbial saying that "Rinzai is for a general, and Sōtō for a farmer". In this way Zen led to the cult of *Bushido*, the "Way of the Warrior", and this close association with the soldier class is one of the more astonishing transformations of Buddhism. Zen did much to stimulate the innate Japanese sensitiveness to beauty (*mono-no-aware*). As Ch'an had done in China, so Zen in Japan from the end of the Kamakura period onwards greatly stimulated not only architecture, sculpture, painting, calligraphy and pottery, but also poetry and music. The close bonds between Zen and the Japanese national character have often been stressed. Buddhist literature was further enriched by two new literary forms, the Noh drama and the so-called "farewell songs". In a culture dominated by the Samurai, death was an ever-present reality, and to overcome the fear of death became one of the purposes of Zen training. Under the Ashikaga Shoguns (1335–1573) Zen had the support of the government. Its cultural influence was then at its height and it could spread among society in general because it emphasized concrete action rather than speculative thought. Actions must be simple, and yet have depth, and "simple elegance" (*wabi* or *sabi*) became the accepted ideal of conduct. In the sixteenth century the tea ceremony was systematized by Zen masters. At the same time many artists believed that "Zen and art are one", Sesshu (1420–1506) being the best-known among them.

After 1500 things were no longer going so well with Japanese Buddhism. Its creative power had waned, and now its political power was broken. Nobunaga destroyed the Tendai stronghold on Hieizan in 1571, and Hideyoshi the great Shingon centre at Negoro, in 1585. Under the Tokugawa (1603–1867) there was a revival of Confucianism and later on, in the eighteenth century, of militant Shintoism. Buddhism receded into the background, the organization and activities of the monks were carefully supervised by the government, which assured the income of the Church while doing everything to prevent any independent life from developing in it. Buddhism sank into a torpid condition. The traditions of the sects, were, however, maintained. The Zen sect alone showed some vitality. In the seventeenth century Hakuin introduced new life into the Rinzai sect, which regarded him as its second founder; the poet Basho evolved a new style of poetry; and in 1655 a third Zen sect, the Óbaku, was imported from China and has always retained marked Chinese characteristics.

In 1868 Buddhism was to a great extent disendowed and for a short time it seemed that it would die out altogether. After 1890, however, its influence has again increased steadily and in 1950 two-thirds of the population were connected with one or the other of the chief sects. The adaptation to modern life and to the competition with Christianity has gone further than in any other Buddhist country so far. In recent years, Japanese Zen has aroused great interest in Europe and America and in D. T. Suzuki it has found a very fine interpreter.

7 TIBET

About the year 1000 a revival of Buddhism took place, initiated by a few enthusiasts who lived in the utmost East and West of the country, where the pressure of persecution was least felt. They soon re-established contact with India and Kashmir, which some of them visited themselves, and also Indian teachers were again invited. The most outstanding personality among these revivers was Rin-chen bzang-po (958–1055), who was prominent not only as a translator, but also as a builder of temples and monasteries in Western Tibet. Of decisive importance was also the coming of Atíśa in 1042, who left Vikramaśílá at the invitation of the king of Western Tibet, and later on established the Pála Maháyána also in Central Tibet. The year 1076 saw a great council in mTho-ling, in West Tibet, where lamas from all parts of Tibet met, and this year can be regarded as marking the final establishment of Buddhism in Tibet.

Atíśa's services were not confined to the re-establishment of the religion throughout the length and breadth of the country. He also created a system of chronology which is still used in Tibet, and which defines each year by its position in a cycle of sixty years, which results from combining five elements, viz. earth, iron, water, wood and fire with the twelve animals of the zodiac, i.e. dog, boar, mouse, ox, tiger, hare, dragon, serpent, horse, sheep, monkey and bird. Without this chronological system the work of the historians, which later on forms one of the glories of Tibetan literature, would have been impossible. This was not all. It is one of the difficulties of Buddhism as a doctrine that it is so profuse in its teachings and methods, that a guide to them and a classification is desirable. Atíśa provided this in his "Lamp illuminating the road to enlightenment", in which he distinguishes the practices according to three levels of spiritual development. The lowest are those who seek happiness in this world and consider only their own interest; the second are those who are also intent on their own interest, but more intelligently, by leading a virtuous life, and seeking for purification; the last are those who have the salvation of all at heart. The full fruits of this manual came only 300 years later, with Tsong-kha-pa.

The next four hundred years saw the formation of Tibetan sects, founded by Tibetans themselves and adjusted to their mental and social conditions. Each of them excelled in one of the things which make up the Buddhist spiritual life. The sects differ in their monastic organization, in their dress, in the tutelary deities, in their interpretation of the Ádi-Buddha, in the methods of meditation they prefer and so on. But they have interacted on one another, and much mutual borrowing has taken place.

The first of these sects were the *Bka-gdam-pa*, founded by 'Brom ston, a pupil of Atíśa, about 1050. They derived their name from the fact that they followed the "authoritative word" of Atíśa as laid down in his book on the "Road to Enlightenment". They represent the central tradition of Tibetan Buddhism, and form the link between the Indian pandits of the first period and the Yellow Church which dominated Tibet after 1400. They paid great attention to morality and monastic discipline, were strictly celibate, and produced many saintly and learned men.

A much closer contact with the life of the people was achieved by the *bKa-rgyud-pa*. Founded by Mar-pa (1012–97) they became in the course of time the most Tibetan of all the sects. For some time they possessed some worldly power, but always less than the Saskyapa and Gelugpa. They aimed not so much at theoretical knowledge as at its practical realization. They are still one of the strongest "unreformed" sects, and regard marriage as no bar to sanctity. The biographies of their teachers show us no stock saints, but human beings as they actually are, with all their imperfections and foibles. From their ranks came Mila-ras-pa (1040–1123), Tibet's greatest and most popular saint and poet, a direct disciple of Marpa. Everyone in Tibet has heard some of his famous "One Hundred Thousand" songs, and everyone is familiar with the main events of his life.

How he learned the black arts and revenged himself on his family's enemies by making a house collapse on them, and smashing their fields with a hailstorm. How he soon realized his guilt, feared to be reborn in hell, and sought purification by the "direct methods" of the Vajrayána. How in his 38th year he found Marpa, who for six years tormented him, so as to allow him to work off his evil deeds. How, when he was 44, he was held ripe for initiation, and how he then spent the remaining 39 years of his life as a hermit on the high Himalayas near the Nepalese border, or wandering about and converting people, until he died from drinking poisoned milk, the gift of a jealous lama. Some of the most dramatic scenes of his life took place in the first years after his initiation, when he lived alone in a cave, ate only herbs until he turned green, and never wore more than his thin cotton cloth in the icy cold of the winter. His indifference to property and comfort, as well as his benevolence towards all that lives, never left him. The rich literature of this sect consists largely of short books aiming at teaching the practice of various kinds of Yoga. In their desire to be practical they have always given special attention to *gtum-mo*, the art of creating "magical heat", without which life in the hermitages would be impossible. This is also something which the average person can appreciate, and which can convince him of the truth and effectiveness of Yoga.

A special form of the Prajñápáramitá doctrine was confined to a small elite, to the *Shi-byed-pa* ("The Pacifiers") founded about 1090, who had a far greater religious than social significance. They were less well organized than the other sects, and consisted of loose groups of Yogins or hermits or mystics, who devoted themselves to solitary meditation. Their teaching was originally inspired by Pha-dam-pa, an Indian teacher from South India, who in his turn owed much to the doctrines of

Áryadeva, the Mádhyamika. It is a Tantric adaptation of the essential spiritual message of Buddhism. The spiritual life consists of two stages: (1) purification, by cutting off the passions, and (2) pacification, which consists in the removal of all suffering and the attainment of even-mindedness. For the first they relied on meditational practices which aimed at driving away the evil spirits which tempt us to commit unwholesome thoughts and for the second they relied largely on the repetition of mantras, such as that of the "Heart Sútra" which appeases all ill, or of short sayings, such as "illness", "joy", "death", and "pleasure". The greater splendours of priestly power should not blind us to the quiet work of these unworldly people.

More worldly were the *Sa-skya-pa*, who derive their name from the monastery of Saskya which had been founded in 1073. They provided the counterweight to the Bka-gdam-pa and Shi-byed-pa by excelling in social organization. After the destruction of the monarchy, Tibet was without a central authority. The Saskya abbots now took over the reins of government, each one handing the rule to his sons. 'Phags-pa (1235–80) was one of the most prominent among these new hereditary rulers of the whole of Tibet and his position as such was recognized by the emperor Khubilai. The sect has produced many men of great learning, it is still in existence, but it lost its worldly power long ago. The power was bought by an increase in worldliness and the monks of the great monasteries, like those of Japan at the same time, formed themselves into great hordes who fought battles among themselves, sacked each other's monasteries, and behaved in a manner unworthy of their professed teachings.

We are not really sufficiently informed about the very powerful *Nying-ma-pa* sect, the followers of Padmasambhava, to know how they survived the long persecution. Quite

131

possibly many of them did so in the guise of Bon priests. Nor can we be sure what in their doctrines is actually due to later developments and what to Padmasambhava himself. The organization of the sect seems to go back to 1250, and is the work of Gu-ru Chos dbyang. The Nyingmapas themselves distinguish two stages of their tradition, the sayings (*bka'-ma*) of the Indian masters, and the "Buried Treasures" (*gter-ma*), which were scriptures hidden by Padmasambhava or the Ádibuddha. Between 1150 and 1550 a considerable number of *gtermas* were unearthed, and their discovery made it easy to camouflage religious innovation. The biography we have of Padmasambhava was thus "discovered" about 1350. Many of these *gtermas* do, however, preserve traditions of great antiquity, as is particularly obvious in the famous "Book of the Dead" (*bar do thos grol*).

The Nyingmapa distinguish six kinds of *bardo*, or of experiences which are "intermediary" in the sense that they are somewhere in between this world of ordinary sensory awareness on the one hand, and the purely spiritual realm of Nirvana on the other. The first three occur (1) in the womb during the months which precede birth, (2) in certain kinds of controlled dreams, and (3) during deep trance. The other three *bardos* are in addition "intermediary" in the sense that they take place in the interval between death and reconception, which is said to last forty-nine days (see p. 34). During that time the ordinary physical body is replaced by a kind of subtle or "ethereal" body. The "Book of the Dead" graphically describes in some detail the visions which are likely to befall those steeped in the traditions of Lamaism during that period. This work has preserved some of the ancient Stone-age knowledge about life after death and shows surprising similarities to other traditions found in Egyptian, Persian and Christian writings.

Very old is also the ceremony of *gCod*, about which we know from a description of a fourteenth century author, and which aims at "cutting off" all attachment to self by offering one's body to the greedy demons on a lonely and deserted site.

The Nyingmapa differ from the other sects in that they utilize that which is generally discarded, like anger or lust, and also the physical body, which is generally looked upon as a shackle and a source of evil, is used here as a means to further an enriched life of the spirit. On the whole their ideas are in keeping with those of the left-handed Tantra in India. The order of their practice is (1) the mental creation of tutelaries (*yi-dam*) with the help of mantras, visions and the "sky walkers" (see p. 79); (2) the control of the occult body, with its arteries, semen virile, etc.; (3) the realization of the true nature of one's own mind. Samantabhadra, the celestial Bodhisattva corresponding to Vairocana, is the source of the highest revelation about the third stage. "Suchness, including yourself, is not intrinsically entangled – so why should you try to disentangle yourself? It is not intrinsically deluded – so why should you seek the truth apart from it?" The repression involved in Buddhist morality is thus rejected. A well-rounded personality does not suppress lust, anger, etc., but puts them into their proper place. In its highest teachings this school has great affinity with the Ch'an sect, in that the highest form of Yoga consists in realizing the true nature of one's own mind. Like the Ch'an school it also speaks of enlightenment in a somewhat non-Indian sense (see p. 99). The man who has won Nirvana here and now, and whose actions are free from causation, is able to make his body vanish in a rainbow. The Nyingmapa concentrated on esoteric teaching and personal realization, and preferred intuitive insight to communicable knowledge. Until about a century ago they had no academic studies in the Gelugpa sense. Then they were in some places introduced in imitation of their rivals.

This sect has continually struggled for power against the others, and although it has several times attempted to gain control of the country, it could never hold it. This was due less to the greater spiritual power of their more virtuous rivals, than to their superior political gifts. So great is the hold of the Nyingmapa over the people that the other sects must make concessions to them. Many of their magical practices are suspect to the other Buddhists not so much because they regard them as ineffective, but because they seem to show an undue concern for worldly well-being. When the Gelugpas want to foresee the future, they normally do not do so themselves but employ an oracle-priest belonging to the ranks of the "Ancient Ones". The Nyingmapas have absorbed many Bon teachings, and it is in their midst that Buddhism and Bon continuously interact. The fact that they go down to the lowest has often been held against them. There is, however, no reason to doubt that in spite, or perhaps because, of that they were as capable of winning the highest as their "purer" colleagues were.

The victory over the Nyingmapa finally went to the *Dge-lugs-pa*, "The Virtuous Ones", the sect founded by Tsong-kha-pa (1327–1419), the last great thinker of the Buddhist world. He was a reformer who carried on Atíśa's work, insisted on the observance of the moral precepts and monastic rules, strictly regulated the daily routine of the monks, reduced the weight of magic by stressing the spiritual side of Buddhism and founded the "Yellow Church", which ruled Tibet until 1950. He was a very great scholar and in every way he tried to find a position between the extremes, to avoid one-sidedness and to attain an encyclopaedic universality. His influence was perpetuated by many pupils, by the foundation of rich and powerful monasteries and by the sixteen volumes of his Collected Works. Among these we must mention two compendia which show the way to salvation, the one through the six Maháyánistic perfections, the other through Tantric practices. The first, "The Steps which lead to Enlightenment", is modelled on Atíśa's manual (see p. 129) but greater attention is accorded to those who are not particularly gifted. After his death Tsong-kha-pa became the object of a fervent religious cult, and he is believed to reside now in the Tusita heavens, as future Buddhas do.

Apart from the formation of indigenous schools, three great achievements are to the credit of the Tibetan Buddhism of this period. First there is the *codification of the canonical literature* in two gigantic collections, the Kanjur (*bka-'gyur*) for the Sútras in the thirteenth, and the Tanjur (*bstan 'gyur*) for the Sástras in the fourteenth century. The Kanjur was printed for the first time in Peking about 1411, and both collections were printed in Tibet for the first time in sNarthang in 1731 and 1742 respectively. Many other editions followed, and the Canon in the comprehensive, accurate, authoritative and easily accessible form which it achieved between the thirteenth and eighteenth centuries has formed the backbone of all Buddhist studies in Tibet.

Secondly there is the production of an enormous indigenous literature – of manuals, commentaries, sub-commentaries and so on. In one field of literature the Buddhists of Tibet have excelled all others, and that was the writing of History. This historical interest is connected with the way in which the Tibetans see the development of Buddhism in relation to the historical Buddha. The full import and meaning of the Buddha's Dharma, so they believe, has revealed itself over many centuries, and the many facets of its infinite richness were grasped by His followers only very slowly, over a period of 1,500 years. It is a curious fact that it was not an Indian but a Tibetan who wrote the best history of Buddhism in India. Bu-ston's (1322) "History of Buddhism in India and Tibet" (chos-'byun) is indeed a masterpiece of its kind, comprehensive and marked by deep philosophical understanding. The first volume gives a survey of the Scriptures; the second deals with the "twelve principal events in the life of the Buddha Śākyamuni", followed by the "three rehearsals of the doctrine", and so on up to the "prophecies about the disappearance of the doctrine" in India, and its continuation in Tibet; the third volume gives an introduction to the Narthang edition of the Canon, followed by a systematic table of contents. Many other first-class works deal either with the history of Buddhism in Tibet, or that of the different sects.

Thirdly, the Buddhist Church became firmly rooted in the life of the people. In the course of the fifteenth century the disciples of Tsong-kha-pa adapted to the needs of social organization the old Buddhist doctrine according to which the Buddhas, saints and Bodhisattvas could conjure up phantom bodies, which to all intents and purposes are indistinguishable from ordinary .bodies, and which they use as a kind of puppet to help and convert others. They are in no way "incarnations" of the saint in question, but free creations of his magical power, which he sends out to do his work, while he himself remains uncommitted. In the fifteenth century the Gelugpas gave a concrete form to this teaching by claiming that certain Bodhisattvas (like Avalokiteśvara and Maitreya) and Buddhas (like Amitābha) would send into certain places, such as Lhasa, Urga, and so on, a certain number of phantom bodies (*sprul-sku, Tulku*, see p. 51) to act as their priestly rulers. In addition they thought it possible to rediscover the phantom body of the deceased ruler in a child conceived forty-nine days after his death. The rule of the *Tulkus*, carefully chosen by skilled monks on the basis of rules as elaborate as those which enable the Congregation of Rites to distinguish genuine from spurious miracles, was the distinguishing feature of the Lamaist world during the last 450 years. It brought with it a great measure of social stability and up to 1950 protected Buddhism effectively from the inroads of modern civilization. What is more, Lamaism has proved surprisingly immune against the upsurge of popular cupidity which accompanied the breakdown of the old order in Asia. In Lamaist Ladakh the loyal tenants of monastic lands in 1953 resisted the expropriation of the monks. The Indian State Government sent a Commission which reported that "it was rather surprising that the tenants who were likely to gain by the operation of the Act (abolishing the big landed estates) on the lands attached to the *gumpas* have unanimously decided that these lands should remain attached to the *gumpas* and be free from the operation of the Abolition Act" (pp. 30–1 of the *Report of the Wazir Committee*).

The Buddhists had often before attempted to combine both secular and spiritual power in their hands. This was the first time they succeeded in doing so. The advantages are obvious. Conditions favourable to a religious life can be assured, militarism reduced to a minimum, animals protected, acquisitiveness discouraged, noise and unrest suppressed. The undisputed rule of the Lamas was backed up by the universality of their intellectual interests, which can be seen in the programme of studies pursued by the Gelugpas, by a pantheon which was extensive and comprehensive, and by the omnipresence of the objects of faith.

Nevertheless, in spite of this outward success, a religious decline set in after the seventeenth century. The Great Fifth

Dalai Lama's (1617–1715) habitual reliance on violence boded ill for the future. The Lamaist system gradually became fossilized. Up to the eighteenth century foreign influences had been welcomed and encouraged. From then onwards the country was shut off and this measure not only reflected the policy of the Peking government, but also a certain inward timidity. The decline shows itself clearly in the works of art, which from now on show more mechanical competence than creative genius. Rare, though still discernible, are the traces of the qualities which had marked Tibetan art at its height – with its fire and almost magical fascination, its overpowering compassion and horror, its ethereal lightness and demonic compulsion, and its nearly superhuman skill in the handling of proportions and colours. For a long time geographical inaccessibility and the rivalry of the powers prevented the country from being conquered. Now modern civilization flows in. Roads, medicine, land reform and the development of natural resources have begun their work, with consequences quite disastrous to religious traditions.

8 MONGOLIA

The Mongols were twice converted by the Tibetan hierarchs, first in 1261 by the Saskya ruler 'Phags-pa, then again in 1577 by the Dalai Lama. In the interval between 1368 and 1577 they had reverted to their native shamanism. It was the Tibetans' ability to work magic which most impressed the Mongols. Marco Polo tells us wonderful things about the various magical tricks the Lamas performed at the court of the Great Khan, and later on, when the Dalai Lama journeyed to Altan Chagan, ruler of the Eastern Mongols, he everywhere showed his magical powers, forced rivers to flow uphill, made springs well up in the desert, and the traces of his horse's hooves formed the *Om mani padme húm*. As a result of the Mongol conversion to Buddhism the Lamas took over many of the magical rites which formerly the shamans had performed. Buddhist respect for life was enforced by legislation forbidding the shamanistic sacrifices of women, slaves and beasts, and restricting hunting.

In consequence of the first conversion, Lamaism shared in the wealth of the Mongol Empire, could establish many monasteries and sanctuaries in China, particularly in Peking, and acquired great power under the Yüan dynasty (1260–1368). The second conversion was followed by a religious fervour which shows what hold the Buddhist religion can have over the mind of a nation. There seemed to be no limits to the piety of the Mongol people. The holy scriptures were translated into Mongol and many thousands of often splendid monasteries were built, which contained up to 45 per cent of the male population and were not infrequently centres of considerable intellectual activity. In the thirteenth century the conquest of Iran by the Mongols had led to the establishment of centres of Buddhist culture in Iranian lands for about half a century before the Il-khanid rulers became Muslims in 1295. After their second conversion the Mongols spread Buddhism to other nomadic populations, like the Buryats and Kalmuks. Urga became a great centre of Lamaism. The last Hutuktu died in 1924, and his functions were taken over by the Mongolian People's Republic. For three hundred years the devotion of the Mongols to Buddhism had been distinguished by the intensity of its fervour, and because their deep faith had not counted the cost a certain degree of national exhaustion ensued, as in the parallel case of Korea in the fourteenth century. It is only natural that now they should have turned to something else.

9 THE PRESENT SITUATION

During the last century Buddhism had to spend most of its energies in maintaining itself, not without difficulties, against the driving forces of modern history. Nowhere has it had the initiative. In the 1950s many Asian Buddhists celebrated the 2,500th anniversary of the Buddha's enlightenment, which was known as the "Buddha Jayanti", because it implied His "victory" over Mara, who personifies death, evil and this world. The event was marked by great enthusiasm which did not, however, concern Buddhism as a spiritual but as a social force. More so perhaps even than Europeans, Asians as a mass have at present withdrawn their interests from religious matters. Social and political issues seem to them so much more urgent. Buddhism is the only factor common to all Asian culture, at least from the Indus and Hindu Kush to Kyoto and Java. All those who dwell in Asia can take pride in a religion which is not only five centuries older than that of the West, but has spread and maintained itself with little recourse to violence and has remained unstained by religious wars, holy inquisitions, sanguinary crusades or the burning of women as witches. Nationalistic self-assertion is a prime motive at this stage of history and the achievements of the Buddhists are certainly something to be proud of. India cherishes the Buddha as one of her greatest religious teachers and Aśoka, the Buddhist emperor, as one of her most outstanding rulers. Not only in India, but also in China, Japan and Ceylon, the most brilliant periods of history were precisely those in which Buddhism flourished most. Splendid buildings and works of art in profusion, as well as a vast, subtle and often beautiful literature testify to the continuous outpouring of cultural values of a high order. From the Buddhist point of view all these things are, of course, mere trifles, accidental by-products of intense spiritual contemplation. But they are splendid trifles.

Prophecies dating from the beginning of the Christian era have given 2,500 years as the duration of the teaching of the Buddha Śákyamuni. After that even the monks "will be strong only in fighting and reproving" and the holy doctrine will become more and more invisible. It is also a fact of observation that, like the other traditional religions, Buddhism has suffered severely from the impact of industrial civilization which has nearly completed its work of destruction in the twenty years which have passed since the Buddha Jayanti.

The bulk of the Northern Buddhists have now passed under Communist control – first Outer Mongolia (1924), then China (1949), then Tibet (1950), and finally Indo-China (1945, 1971). The effects of anti-religious totalitarian regimes are bound to be unfavourable. In Mongolia the religion is practically extinct. In China the monks, persecuted already under the Kuomintang, are exhorted to take an interest in the masses, and to live up to their vow to "benefit all living beings" in ways which they had never intended. Buddhist monuments are treated as museum pieces, Buddhist beliefs as deplorable superstitions which, however, are somehow associated with the great days of the T'ang dynasty and of Chien-lung, while also providing valuable links with Japan and other Asian countries.

In Tibet the Dalai Lama had to flee in 1959, taking nearly 70,000 of his supporters with him to India. The holy land of Tibet has ceased to exist, its feudal social structure is being dismantled root and branch, its priestly artefacts, such as books, images and paintings, are destroyed or removed, and its inhabitants ushered into the satisfactions of an industrializing militarized society. Its purpose is no longer to uphold the Faith, but to guard the Chinese People's Republic against attacks from India, the Soviet Union or the United States. The influence of Marxism spreads also further South. Even in Burma and Sri

Lanka many monks are sufficiently in contact with the ordinary "man in the village" to have turned left and to work for a synthesis of Buddhism and Socialism.

On many issues Communists and Buddhists are bound to clash: universal military service is abhorrent, particularly when applied to monks; Buddhist otherworldliness frowns on the uncontrolled growth of applied science and technology; and the mere building of railways, motor roads and airfields, with all that it entails, is detrimental to calm and serenity. The central conflict, however, concerns monastic institutions, without which Buddhism cannot exist. In a society dedicated to the production of material wealth an order of contemplative monks must appear anomalous and parasitical and its economic basis will be pretty precarious. The fate of a harassed and barely tolerated minority — that is what is in store for the Buddhists of those countries. So at least is the outlook on the plane of social reality. On the plane of ideas it may well be different. The doctrinal similarities between Maháyána Buddhism and dialectical materialism are surprisingly close and by a process of osmosis both sides will learn from each other in due course.

Likewise outside the Communist area the damage done has been severe. In their desire to spread the blessings of their plutocratic democracy to the Far East the Americans used all the resources of their technology to devastate first Japan, then Korea, then Vietnam, and after that Laos and Cambodia. The last, in particular, had been quite a showcase of Buddhism. Although a neutral, it was bombed back into the Stone Age, all the refinements of civilization were blotted out and for the time being it has fallen into the hands of rather primitive mountain tribes. In Burma U Nu's shortlived attempt to revive the royal Buddhism of a glorious past was superseded by a humdrum military dictatorship. In Thailand the monarchy and their supporters were so afraid of communists that the country was handed over to a military dictatorship, Buddhist monks were seen to sprinkle holy water on American tanks and tens of thousands of USAF troops were invited to pulverize their neighbours with B-52s. This has assured the ultimate triumph of communism also there.

In Japan our industrial age has put a premium on those sects, Zen, Shin and Nichiren, which have most radically departed from tradition. Shin, the numerically most successful sect, has reduced Buddhist doctrines and practices to a point where they become hardly perceptible. The threatened American invasion of 1853 had been followed twenty years later by the disestablishment of the Buddhist Church and the burning or confiscation of innumerable temples, while the actual invasion of 1945 brought financial ruin to the monasteries through MacArthur's "land reform" of 1947–50, led to a "general trend towards profanity" and to widespread religious apathy. It also brought about an enormous growth of nationalistic Buddhism. The latest census of Japan shows the Nichiren groups to number 30 million out of 75 million Buddhists. Of these more than one half belong to the "True Nichiren Sect", which grew with amazing rapidity from 350,000 members in 1955 to 15,700,000 in 1968. They are lay movements of the Nichiren line, which are run by and for merchants and craftsmen, all humble, common, ordinary people intent on improving the quality of their daily lives. The largest are the Sóka-gakkai, Reiyú-kai and Risshó-kósai-kai, founded respectively in 1930, 1925 and 1938. In appearance and behaviour these people are not unlike Kiwanis or Shriners, though as Japanese they are blessed with better taste and aesthetic judgment and as Maháyána Buddhists they are exposed to the reverberations of a very high spirituality. This is one of Buddhism's more successful attempts to come to terms with the "American Century". One may well doubt whether capitalism has been any more kind to the Buddhists than communism.

On the credit side what is chiefly to be noted is the considerable work done in recent years, in Burma, Thailand, Japan and Ceylon, to keep alive and to revive the ancient methods of meditation. It is in the seclusion of the meditation centres that the old faith will be recharged, and confer new benefits on the world.

While the strongholds of Buddhism in the East were being destroyed one by one, it was some compensation that the religion has slowly but steadily spread to the capitalist countries of the West. There it has been absorbed on three different levels – the philosophical, the scholarly and the sectarian.

1. The philosophical reception began with Arthur Schopenhauer in 1819 and has continued at a fairly steady pace since. Although he had access to very few original documents, Schopenhauer reproduced the Buddhist system of thought from Kantian antecedents with such an accuracy that one may well believe that he remembered it from a previous life. He in his turn greatly influenced musicians like Richard Wagner, philosophers like Bergson, and many other creative people in Western Europe. From quite another angle the genius of Helena Petrovna Blavatsky introduced the West to many of the basic teachings of Maháyána Buddhism and her Theosophical Society has fostered further research in many ways. In more recent years such divers philosophers as Rickert, Jaspers, Wittgenstein and Heidegger have testified to their having been

influenced by Buddhism, and over the last twenty years there has grown up a vast literature on the relationship between various Buddhist thought systems and those of modern European thinkers. It is of such a consistently high quality that it cannot fail to leave its mark on Western, as well as Eastern, philosophical thought. One day the West, tired of being critical, will become creative again; and the East, now so cowed, will once again raise its head.

2. For 150 years the countless documents of Buddhist history, whether literary or artistic, have attracted the attention of many scholars. To some extent this interest was prompted by the administrative needs of imperialist governments who found Buddhists among their newly conquered subjects. In this way the Russians came to study the views of their Siberian Buddhists; puzzled by the Ceylonese attitude to land tenure the English in Ceylon, among them the Rhys Davids, turned to their religious books for an answer; the French did exceptionally fine work through the École Française d'Extrême Orient which was based on Saigon; lately even the Americans had attached to their Army a school of Oriental languages which first trained many of the Orientalists now at work in American universities, whose graduate students live on grants from the N(ational) D(efence) E(xpense) A(ccount), and who are heavily subsidized by CIA, FBI and the large Foundations. But this was not all. Just as Buddhism proved to be the most exportable form of Indian culture, so no form of Asian thinking has evoked more interest in Europe. No other religion has attracted such a galaxy of scholarly talent, not only first-class philologists drawn to the often difficult languages in which the Buddhists expressed themselves, but first-class minds bent on interpreting the subtleties and profundities of Buddhist thought. It took a long time to get to the bottom of Buddhist

thinking or to even understand the terminology they employed. At first we were in the position of Egyptologists who, with all the priests dead, have to guess wildly and who have managed to reduce to a farrago of absurdities what to the best Greeks was the highest wisdom. Likewise to the first interpreters – proconsuls, missionaries, military men and financial administrators – the Buddhist religion seemed to be ludicrous nonsense. There were a few exceptions, of course, like R. C. Childers (*c.* 1870), and, following in his footsteps, after a time the proud conquerors of Asia unbent and tried to learn from Buddhist monks who survived in Japan, Ceylon and Siberia. By the 1930s things began to fall into shape, and we can now be fairly confident to catch the spiritual meaning which the Buddhist authors wished to convey.

3. From the stratospheric heights of philosophy and the mountainous terrain of scholarship we now descend to the low-flying flatlands of popular sectarian Buddhism. Buddhist societies have sprung up for nearly eighty years, chiefly in Protestant countries. There they form one of the smaller Non-conformist sects. They try to outshine active Christian Love with their more non-violent *Mettá*, to determine the meaning of the Holy Scriptures from often inaccurate English translations without much recourse to the originals, and to add meditation and some exotic glamour to good works, a blameless life and a ceaseless denigration of the intellect. Over the last twenty years these groups and conventicles have rapidly grown in numbers and financial weight. At first they took their inspiration almost exclusively from what they could learn about the Páli scriptures which, as good Protestants, they believed to be the original Gospel, the Buddha-dhamma in its pristine purity; then, in the wake of the magnificent publications of Daisetz Taitaro Suzuki in the thirties, there has been a flood of

what describes itself as "Zen"; Conze and others added a fuller knowledge of the Prajñápáramitá and other early Maháyána texts; and since 1950 there have been many attempts to add also some Tantra to the mixture. In America side by side with the organized Buddhist groups a few gifted individuals, like Alan Watts and Gary Snyder, liberally scattered a variety of unco-ordinated ideas like seed-pods in all directions. In the sixties they had some influence on the "counter culture" which fed on the revulsion against the strains of a technological consumer society and the horrors of the war in Vietnam. Generally speaking, however, sectarian Buddhists keep themselves to themselves and have little impact on the world in general. No one can at present estimate their potentialities. Everything about them is obscure – whether it be their numbers, their financial resources, the social origin of their members, their motivation, their spiritual maturity, their doctrinal stance or the range of their influence. So why pry into the future?

Disinterestedness and self-effacement have been the most effective weapons of the Buddhists in the past. They would sadly depart from the outlook of their spiritual forebears if now they were to start worrying about whether Buddhist institutions can maintain a foothold in our present world. When asked "how a drop of water could be prevented from ever drying up", the Buddha replied, "by throwing it into the sea". It is for sayings such as this that he has been revered as the Enlightened One.

BIBLIOGRAPHY

BUDDHISM IN GENERAL

Bu-ston, *History of Buddhism*, trsl. H. Obermiller, 2 vols, 1931–2. – A. Coomaraswamy, *Buddha and the Gospel of Buddhism* (1916), ed. L. Coomaraswamy, 1964. – E. Conze, *Buddhism*, 1951. – R. Robinson, *The Buddhist Religion*, 1970. – J. B. Pratt, *The Pilgrimage of Buddhism*, 1928. – E. Conze, *Buddhist Scriptures*, 1959. – E. Conze, I. B. Horner, D. Snellgrove, A. Waley, *Buddhist Texts through the Ages*, 1954. – S. Beyer, *The Buddhist Experience*, 1974.

BASIC CONCEPTS

Bh. Nyanatiloka, *The Word of the Buddha*, 9th ed., 1948. – E. Conze, *Buddhist Meditation*, 1956. – *Buddhist Thought in India*, 1962. – K. N. Jayatilleke, *Early Buddhist Theory of Knowledge*, 1963. – L. de la Vallée Poussin, *Nirvana*, 1925. – H. V. Guenther, *Philosophy and Psychology in the Abhidharma*, 1957.

ART

D. Seckel, *The Art of Buddhism*, 1963 (Bibl.). – A. Coomaraswamy, *The Elements of Buddhist Iconography*, 1935. – E. Gombaz, L'évolution du Stúpa en Asie, in: *Mélanges Chinois et Bouddhiques*, 1932–6. – J. Eracle, *L'Art des Thanka et le Bouddhisme Tantrique*, 1970. – D. L. Snellgrove, ed. *The Image of the Buddha*, 1977.

INDIA

The first period: E. Lamotte, *Histoire du Bouddhisme Indien*. 1958. – E. J. Thomas, *The Life of the Buddha as Legend and History*, 1927. – A. Foucher, *La Vie du Bouddha*, 1949. – H. Oldenberg, *Buddha*, 13th ed., ed. H. von Glasenapp, 1959. – A. Bareau, *Les Sectes Bouddhiques du Petit Véhicule*, 1955. – E. Mookerji, *Asoka*, 3rd ed., 1962. – G. Woodcock, *The Greeks in India*, 1966.

The second period: Har Dayal, *The Bodhisattva Doctrine in Buddhist Sanskrit Literature*, 1932. – N. Dutt, *Aspects of Mahayana Buddhism*, 1930. – D. T. Suzuki, *Studies in the Lankavatara Sutra*, 1930. – *On Indian Mahayana Buddhism* (ed. E. Conze), 1968. – T. R. V. Murti, *The Central Philosophy of Buddhism*, 1955. – R. Robinson, *Early Madhyamika in India and China*, 1966. – E. Lamotte, *Le Traité de la Grande Vertu de Sagesse*, 5 vols, 1944–79. – *The Travels of Fah-hien*, trsl. H. A. Giles, 1876. – Th. Watters, *On Yuan Chwang's Travels in India*, 2 vols, 1904–5.

The third period: S. B. Dasgupta, *Obscure Religious Cults as Backgrounds of Bengali Literature*, 2nd ed., 1962. – *An Introduction to Tantric Buddhism*, 1950. –

G. Tucci, *Tibetan Painted Scrolls*, 2 vols, 1949 (esp. vol. I, 209–249). – *The Theory and Practice of the Mandala*, 1961. – D. L. Snellgrove, *The Hevajra Tantra*, 2 vols, 1959. – H. Guenther, *Jewel Ornament of Liberation*, (Sgam-po-pa), 1959. – P. Mus, *Barabudur*, 2 vols, 1935. – Th. Stcherbatsky, *Buddhist Logic*, 2 vols, 1930–2.

The fourth period: R. C. Mitra, *The Decline of Buddhism in India*, 1954.

NEPAL

D. L. Regmi, *Ancient Nepal*, 1960. – S. Kramrisch, *The Art of Nepal*, 1964.

KASHMIR

J. N. and P. N. Ganhar, *Buddhism in Kashmir and Ladakh*, 1956.

CEYLON

W. Rahula, *History of Buddhism in Ceylon: the Anuradhapura Period*, 1956. – E. W. Adikaram, *Early History of Buddhism in Ceylon*, 1946. – B. L. Smith, *Tradition and Change in Theravada Buddhism*, 1973. – R. F. Gombrich, *Precept and Practice: Traditional Buddhism in the Rural Highlands of Ceylon*, 1971. – W. Rahula, *The Heritage of the Bhikkhu*, 1974.

SOUTH-EAST ASIA

G. Coedès, *Indianized States of Indo-China and Indonesia*, 1968. – R. C. Lester, *Theravada Buddhism in South East Asia*, 1973. – G. E. Harvey, *History of Burma*, 1925. – S. J. Tambiah, *World Conqueror and World Renouncer*, 1976. – N. Ray, *Sanskrit Buddhism in Burma*, 1936. – R. Butwell, *U Nu of Burma*, 2nd ed. 1970. – E. Sarkisyanz, *Buddhist Backgrounds of the Burmese Revolution*, 1965. – D. E. Smith, *Religion and Politics in Burma*, 1968. – H. H. Prince Dhani-Nivat, *A History of Buddhism in Siam*, 1965. – K. Wells, *Thai Buddhism, Its Rites and Activities*, 1960. – J. Hamilton-Merritt, *A Meditator's Diary*, 1976. – A. H. Brodrick, *Little Vehicle: Cambodia and Laos*, 1949.

CENTRAL ASIA

A. Stein, *Serindia*, 5 vols, 1921. – A. Giles, *Six Centuries at Tun Huang*, 1944. – K. Saha, *Buddhism and Buddhist Literature in Central Asia*, 1970. – P. Demiéville, *Récents Travaux sur Touen-Houang*, 1970.

CHINA

K. S. Ch'en, *Buddhism in China* (Bibl.), 1964. – E. Zuercher, *The Buddhist Conquest of China*, 2 vols, 2nd ed. 1972. – Fung Yu-lan, *A History of Chinese Philosophy*, II, 1953, 237–433. – W. Liebenthal, *Chao Lun. The Treatises of Seng-chao*, 1968. – D. T. Suzuki, *Essays in Zen Buddhism*, 3 vols, 1927–32. – H. Dumoulin, *A History of Zen Buddhism*, 1963. – J. Gernet, *Les Aspects Economiques du Bouddhisme dans la Société Chinoise du 5e au 10e Siècles*, 1956. – J. Prip-Møller,

Chinese Buddhist Monasteries, 1937. – H. Welch, *The Practice of Chinese Buddhism, 1900–1950*, 1967. – A. Wright, *Buddhism in Chinese History*, 1959.

KOREA

C. Osgood, *The Koreans and Their Culture*, 1951. – F. Starr, *Korean Buddhist History*, 1918.

JAPAN

Ch. Eliot, *Japanese Buddhism*, 1935. – Steinilber-Oberlin, *The Buddhist Sects of Japan*, 1938. – D. T. Suzuki, *Zen and Japanese Culture*, 1959. – M. W. de Visser, *Ancient Buddhism in Japan*, 2 vols, 1928, 1935. – H. Nakamura, *Ways of Thinking of Eastern Peoples: India-China-Tibet-Japan*, 1964. – M. Anesaki, *Nichiren, the Buddhist Prophet*, 1916. – N. Brannen, *Soka Gakkai*, 1968.

TIBET

H. Hoffman, *The Religions of Tibet*, 1961. – C. Ben, *The Religion of Tibet*, 1931. – P. Demiéville, *Le Concile de Lhasa*, 1952. – H. W. Evans-Wentz, *Tibet's Great Yogi Milarepa*, 1928. – *The Hundred Thousand Songs of Milarepa*, trsl. Garma C. C. Chang, 2 vols, 1962. – G. Roerich, *The Blue Annals*, 2 vols, 1949–53. – D. L. Snellgrove, *Buddhist Himalayas*, 1957.

MONGOLIA

S. Camman, *The Land of the Camel*, 1951. – E. D. Philips, *The Mongols*, 1969. – C. R. Bawden, *The Jebtsundampa Khutuktus of Urga*, 1961.

EUROPE AND AMERICA

H. de Lubac, *La Rencontre du Bouddhisme et de l'Occident*, 1952. – J. W. de Jong, *A Brief History of Buddhist Studies in Europe and America*, 1976. – W. Peiris, *The Western Contribution to Buddhism*, 1973. – E. McCloy Layman, *Buddhism in America*, 1976. – C. Humphreys, *Sixty Years of Buddhism in England*, 1968. – I. P. Oliver, *Buddhism in Britain*, 1979.

COMPARATIVE STUDIES

K. N. Upadhyaya, *Early Buddhism and the Bhagavad Gita*, 1971. – J. E. Carpenter, *Buddhism and Christianity*, 1923. – J. W. Boyd, *Satan and Mara. Christian and Buddhist Symbols of Evil*, 1975. – C. Gudmunsen, *Wittgenstein and Buddhism*, 1977.

Most of the books mentioned have been reprinted several times. The date given is that of the first publication, except where I believe that one particular edition is preferable.

The books in French cover essential topics which no one has adequately treated in English.

Further study will, of course, involve the original documents. If these are read in translation one should remember that they are rarely accurate if made before 1940, by which date Buddhist terminology was at last being understood.

INDEX